MANAGING TEEN ANGER

AND

VIOLENCE

A Pathways to Peace Program

Also by William Fleeman

The Pathways to Peace Anger Management Workbook (2003)

The Pathways to Sobriety Workbook (2004)

The Niagara Falls Metaphor (video, 2002)

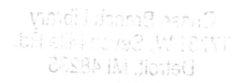

MANAGING TEEN ANGER

AND

VIOLENCE

A Pathways to Peace Program

William Fleeman

Manassas Park, VA

MANAGING TEEN ANGER AND VIOLENCE

A Pathways to Peace Program

ISBN: 1-57023-276-8 (10-digit)
         978-1-57023-276-3 (13-digit)

Library of Congress Number: 2007940057

Publisher: For information on Impact Publications, including current and forthcoming publications, authors, press kits, online bookstore, and submission requirements, visit Impact's website: www.impactpublications.com.

Publicity/Rights: For information on publicity, author interviews, and subsidiary rights, contact the Public Relations Department, Tel. 703-361-7300, Fax 703-335-9486, or e-mail: query@impactpublications.com.

Sales/Distribution: All bookstore sales are handled through Impact's trade distributor, National Book Network, 15200 NBN Way, Blue Ridge Summit, PA, 17214, Tel. 1-800-462-6420. All other sales and distribution inquiries should be directed to the publisher: IMPACT PUBLICATIONS, 9104 Manassas Drive, Suite N, Manassas Park, VA 20111-5211, Tel. 703-361-7300, Fax 703-335-9486, or e-mail: query@impactpublications.com.

CONTENTS

Part III: *Changing Your Behavior*

Part IV: *Changing Your Mindset*

Appendix

DEDICATION

In loving memory of my oldest son Nate, one of the lost.

In loving appreciation of my youngest son Will, one of the found.

To my wonderful wife and superb first-line editor: my deepest love
and appreciation.

Honorable mention and thanks to Dustin, Olivia, and John Valenti: for your
superb technical assistance.

MANAGING TEEN ANGER AND VIOLENCE

A Pathways to Peace Program

INTRODUCTION

To Parents, Counselors, and Teachers

Managing Teen Anger and Violence: A Pathways to Peace Program is an anger management and violence prevention guidebook designed specifically for young people age 13 to 19. It is an interactive guide to help teens understand, and then change their angry behavior. The lessons and exercises in the workbook follow a logical sequence. The readability level of Managing Teen Anger and Violence makes the material accessible to most teens. This book is the official guide for teens who participate in the Pathways to Peace, Inc. anger management and violence prevention self-help program. Pathways to Peace, Inc. is a nonprofit organization based in New York State, with community-based groups throughout the U.S. and Canada. The guidebook is designed so that it may be used by teens regardless of whether or not they participate in a Pathways to Peace anger management group.

Managing Teen Anger and Violence can be used by individuals with or without adult supervision. The workbook can also be used by agencies, institutions, and schools as a curriculum guide for teen anger management and violence prevention programs. A special Master Package of Managing Teen Anger and Violence is available from Pathways to Peace, Inc. The Master Package includes the guidebook inside a loose-leaf binder, along with a DVD which supports some of the key concepts of the Pathways to Peace anger management program. For details on ordering the Master Package, call 1-800-775-4212.

The *Managing Teen Anger and Violence* guidebook is designed to be completed in as little as 16 to 18 one-hour weekly sessions. However, a program of almost any length could be designed. For example, a program could be planned with a completion target of six months to a year.

To Teens Who Want to Change Their Angry Behavior

This guidebook is only a beginning. Recovery from an anger problem takes longer than a few months, since full recovery requires more than a change in behavior. It could be said that changing angry behavior is the easy part. Changing at the character level takes much longer and requires firm commitment and patience. True recovery will occur when you begin to change at the character level. Full recovery from a long-standing pattern of anger and rage could take as long as two to three years. *Maintaining recovery is an ongoing process*. Work hard. Have patience. Be forgiving of yourself.

Scattered throughout this guidebook are messages written by young people like you. The messages are designed to help you to understand and to relate to the material contained in this book. The young people who wrote the messages have shared their experiences with you because they *care*. Writing down their stories was not easy. They had to remember things and events they would rather not think about. They struggled through the pain. It is very likely that you will relate, not only to the content of the messages, but to the feelings behind the messages too.

Like you, the young people who wrote down their stories have dealt with anger and rage. They once felt alone and powerless. Some have suffered serious consequences because of their behavior. Each writer once thought no one cared. But the young people who have shared parts of their personal history in this guidebook haven't struggled in vain only to lose in the end. They have struggled and won. They found help for their anger problem. They found acceptance and support, and they learned skills to help them deal with anger triggers. They learned how to live in harmony with their families, their friends, and their teachers. Their struggle to change was not easy. Yet, they succeeded. They changed their angry behavior and now are enjoying the rewards. They are living happy, productive lives. Many of them continue to learn and grow by participating in a Pathways to Peace self-help group in their community. To every teen who told part of his or her story and contributed so much to the success of this anger management guidebook for teens, I salute you. I say: "Thank You!"

There are no guarantees, of course. But if you follow the example of the teens who wrote down their messages for you, and if you apply the skills and ideas presented in this guidebook to your life, you can change your angry behavior, avoid further consequences, and find your pathway to peace. Eventually, along the way, you may even find the happy and contented life that you deserve.

Why Some Teens Develop a Problem With Anger

The reasons that some teens develop a problem with anger are many and varied. The main reason given by most teens seems to be an overriding feeling of powerlessness. Teens with anger problems feel powerless over many areas of their life. Underneath this overriding feeling of powerlessness, there are other feelings which are connected to the feeling of powerlessness. Teens with anger problems also feel insecure and unprotected. They feel afraid and sometimes depressed. In other words, teens with anger problems experience most of the same kinds of feelings that all teens feel—in fact the same kinds of feelings that all human beings experience at times. But teens who develop problems with anger often experience these feelings much more strongly.

Another major cause of excessive anger is a feeling of heightened inner tension. Many, but not all, teens who suffer from excessive anger grew up in surroundings that almost inevitably caused them to develop a level of inner tension which is much higher than normal. There are certain conditions that are associated with higher-than-normal levels of inner tension in teens. Poverty is certainly a factor. Overcrowded housing is another. Increased tension levels also result for teens whose parents separate or become divorced. As you will learn, teens with anger problems use anger to relieve excessive inner tension.

Street Gangs and Teen Anger

The first street gangs sprang up in the overcrowded tenement house district of

---

MESSAGE FROM SEAN

Hi. My name is Sean and I'm nineteen. I had a serious anger problem, but I've been working hard at changing. I've made a lot of progress, but I'm still working on it. You know, I'm still puttin' on the finishing touches. Still tweaking my program. You'll be hearing more from me—a lot more—beginning with Chapter One, where I wrote my story down for you.

Maybe you think you're the only teenager in the world with a serious anger problem. But, believe me, you're are not alone. There's me, for example. I have an anger problem too. But I'm working on it. Maybe you think everyone has given up on you. But you're wrong. Not everyone has given up on you. Maybe you've suffered some serious consequences because of your angry behavior. So have I, so have lots of other teens. Maybe you got expelled from school once, maybe more than once, and placed in an alternative education program. You might even have been sent to a detention center. Maybe that's where you are right now, as you read these words. Maybe you feel full of guilt and shame right now, that you've come to believe no one could possibly care whether you live or die. Back when I was getting in so much trouble, that's how I felt. But don't you believe it! It's not true. There are those who care. I care. Otherwise I wouldn't take the time to say this. Chances are, a lot of people care. Your mom or dad, your grandma or grandpa. Your brother, maybe, or your sister. Or some of your friends. Your teachers—all these people, I bet some of them care. The other teens who wrote down parts of their stories in this workbook care. The guy who wrote this book cares.

Sean

New York City in the mid-1800s. Jacob Riis, a NYC investigative reporter, made the first study of street gangs as part of his book *How the Other Half Lives*, written in 1890. Street gangs are now a part of all larger cities in the U.S., as well as in most other countries, and owe their existence to the same reasons Riis cited in his book more than a hundred years ago: poverty and overcrowding, alcoholism and drug addiction, separation and divorce.

Teens join gangs for a variety of reasons. They join gangs in order to feel secure, to feel safe, to feel protected, and to feel accepted. There is one other major reason teens join gangs: anger. Teens who join gangs are angry. Gangs give teens an opportunity to use anger and violence in situations that protect them from the consequences of their behavior. They can engage in fights with rival gangs, or with members of their own gang, without fear of being caught or arrested at the time. Gangs have rules. One of the rules gangs live by is the no-snitch rule. As in the gangs of New York City a hundred years ago, the penalty for snitching is often severe. Those who snitch may be beaten. In some cases, they may even be killed. Gangs are social organizations. They reinforce the angry behavior of gang members. Teens who join gangs are much more likely to commit violent acts, and much less likely to stop their angry behavior. They are also much more likely to go to prison and to suffer premature violent death.

If you are a teen with an anger problem, you should think twice about joining a gang. If you are a gang member already, you should find a way to safely leave the gang behind. Depending on the rules of your gang, this could be difficult. Some gangs have a no-quit rule. A no-quit rule means that you cannot drop your membership in the gang without suffering severe consequences, such as a beating.

William Fleeman
October 2007

PART ONE

Understanding the Problem

CHAPTER ONE
Sean's Story

The first thing you will be asked to do when you begin this book is to do a self-assessment. To "assess" means to take an honest look. To "self-assess" means to take an honest look at yourself. It is time, now, to take an honest look at yourself as a person with an anger problem. But before you begin this tall order, first read Sean's story. Sean has been in Pathways to Peace for a while now, and his life is moving in a direction he would never have thought possible when he started the program. When Sean was asked to share his story with all of you, he said, "Yes, if anybody can find some stuff in my story that they can relate to, well maybe that'll encourage them to hang in there."

Sean isn't the writer's real name. It is the name he chose to use throughout this guidebook, because for obvious reasons he could not use his real name. Nor will he call other people in his story by their real names. Sean will not say exactly where he once lived, nor where he now lives. The events he talks about are real, but exactly where the events happened and exactly who else besides himself might have been involved will be known only to Sean. Before he begins his story, he wants to share something with you which both he and I believe to be important.

Introduction

Hi, I'm Sean. Before I get started on my story, I want you to know about my style. I mean my writing style. Actually, I have more than one. I have one style for letters and emails and one for writing formal stuff like book reports and term papers. The style I'll use for my story, and for messages like this one that'll show up throughout this book,

---

is the one I use when I write emails to my friends. Call it my email style. It's mostly casual in tone, written the way I talk, without too many big words or long complex sentences. I'm not trying to impress anybody, just communicate. Bill, the author of this book, and I argued about what style I should use. He thought I should use a more formal style. He also said no profanity, not even for the sake of communicating better. *"Oh no!"* I said. *"I don't want my story to sound like a *&%# book report!"* Lucky for me, Bill's not too set in his ways (for a guy his age). We compromised. I said I'd throw out all the four-letter words if he'd accept a less formal style of writing. He said okay. So everything I write that you'll read anywhere in this book will be written in my email style. Later, you'll be asked to write your story. I think you'll feel more natural if you use your email style when you write it. By the way, why did I write down my story in this guidebook? I wrote down my story because I want to help—that's right. So laugh in my face, see if I care. Okay, here's my story.

My age, where I was born, and all that...

I'm only nineteen, still under twenty, so you can trust me, right? I was born in a big city on the East Coast, moved to Minnesota when I was five, then to northern California when I was seven, after my mom and dad split up.

My mom and I moved around a lot in the San Francisco Bay area till I was thirteen, then we moved to Southern California. I was always changing schools, making new friends, then leaving. I hated that—the moving around all the time.

My father and mother, sisters and brothers . . .

Both my dad and mom had drug problems. My dad was an alcoholic—a juice head, my mom used to call him. He used drugs too, cocaine and marijuana. My mom was a crackhead. She had a big-time problem with crack. I'm the only kid in my family. I mean, I'm the only child born to my mom and dad. I had a half brother, no sisters half or otherwise. My half brother was a lot older than me. He lived with his mom. I never got to know him, and I'm glad. My dad said my half brother was addicted to meth. He was mental too—too much meth. My dad told Mom he got sent to treatment a bunch of times, ended up in a group home in Atlanta. There were seven or eight other guys living there. All of them, including my half brother, were on Social Security Disability because of mental problems and drugs. Late one night a fire broke out in the group home. It might have been caused when my half brother and some other guys staying in the house cooked up a batch of meth and caught the place on fire. Nobody will ever know, for sure, exactly what happened. The group home was unlicensed and unsupervised—in other words, illegal. And there were no smoke alarms and no fire extinguishers. All the person who owned the house did was collect the rent—$4,000 a month. He didn't care. Four guys burned to death in the fire. My half brother was one of them. That's why I'm glad I never got to know him.

Bad things that happened to me and how they made me feel…

My mom was using crack when she was pregnant with me, so I was born addicted to cocaine. That's the first bad thing that happened to me. Just before I was born, my mom told the doctors about her crack habit, so they treated me for infant withdrawal syndrome. I was lucky I didn't end up with some permanent damage, like some kids who are born addicted to cocaine.

The second bad thing that happened—like I said, my mom and dad split up when I was seven. I didn't think much about it at first. My mom and dad fought all the time. My dad didn't beat on my mom or anything, and he didn't beat on me either. They did a lot of yelling and my dad threw things and broke things, stuff like that. My mom did it too sometimes, I mean she threw things and broke things—lamps, dishes, things like that. It made me feel afraid. Actually, I felt afraid most of the time. If you grew up in a house like mine, I guess you can relate.

So, I thought maybe things would quiet down a little around the apartment and not be so crazy when my dad left. I was wrong. Things quieted down a little at first. But my mom cried a lot, and that made me feel bad. Then she started getting angry a lot. She was in the grief and loss cycle. You'll learn about grief and loss later in the book. After a while, I began to miss my dad. So what if he was a juice head, he was my dad. I missed him. I ended up depressed like my mom, and angry too. For some stupid reason, I used to think it was my fault my mom and dad split up. If your mom and dad split up, maybe like me you think it's your fault—don't! It isn't your fault! It isn't anybody's fault. If alcohol or other drugs were involved, blame the alcohol and drugs. It makes more sense.

My dad was a factory worker. When he left, my mom and I had to go on welfare. Even when my dad was there and was making pretty good money at the factory, we never had much. The dope man and liquor store owner got most of it. I didn't feel too bad about being a welfare kid. Most of my friends came from welfare families too.

The worst thing that ever happened to me

This is the worst thing that ever happened to me. I don't like to talk about it, okay? But it's an important part of my story. It's important because it's the one thing that I'm still fighting to get over. All the counselors always told me it would take a long time. They were right.

I was molested. I even hate to write the word. I was ten years old. The guy owned a little grocery store over by the University. My friends and I didn't hang there, but once in a while I went there to buy an ice cream cone. One day he said he could use some help cleaning up the place after he closed up at the end of the day, and would I like to earn some money? I didn't suspect anything. He seemed all right. I sure could've used some spending money, that's for sure. Anyway, I said, yeah, sure. He said to come back around 6:00 PM, which is when he closed up. I came back and he let me in and handed me a broom. It only took about half an hour to sweep the floor. Then he told me to empty the trash in the dumpster out behind the store. That was it. He said thanks, handed me a $10 bill, and I went home happy. I didn't even work a whole hour. When I got home, I showed my mom the ten I'd earned. She thought it was cool. She'd been in the store before and knew the guy, so she wasn't suspicious either. But she said she thought the dude paid me too much for too little. Next time I went to the store, the guy asked if I'd like to earn another $10. I said sure. When I was done and he handed me the ten, he asked if I'd like to work for him three evenings a week. I told my mom, and she said it'd be okay as long as the job wouldn't keep me out late. Then one night while the owner of the store and I were cleaning up, he went and locked the door early. He said some things had come in by truck earlier in the day and he needed help putting it all away in the stock room out back. That's when it happened.

I was so angry! That sick dude raped me! He robbed me of my self-esteem. He took away my self-worth. He stole my trust. He'd set me up. Okay, that's all I'm going to say right now on the subject. What I've said ain't the half of it. If you've ever been molested or raped, you know there's a lot more to say. And you know how hard it is to say it.

Good things that happened and how they made me feel...

The first good thing I can remember was when my mom got off crack. I mean, stopped smoking crack for good. Oh, she'd been clean from time to time for a couple of weeks, and once for two whole months, when she went to long-term rehab. But she always started up again. One of her crackhead friends would stop over to the apartment, and my mom would start hittin' the pipe again.

One time, when I was ten, I got sent to a foster home. That's another bad thing that happened to me. It was when my mom went to rehab, and the Dept. of Social Services sent me to stay with the Johnsons. The Johnsons treated me all right. I had a nice bedroom all to myself, everything new, my own TV. That was cool. But the Johnsons couldn't take my mom's or my dad's place. Nobody could. Actually, I resented the Johnsons. I resented them because they weren't my real parents. I don't feel that way now, though. They really did help me out. I even go and see them once in a while.

I went back home after my mom got out of rehab. At first, things went okay. But after about a month, my mom picked up the crack pipe again. Then the yelling and screaming started up again, with pots and pans and dishes crashing against the wall. It was just as bad around the apartment as it was when my dad was still there. I didn't hang around the apartment much. I stayed away as much as I could, stayed out as late as I could.

Finally, my mom stopped for good. No rehab this time. She just stopped. Man, she suffered though! She made me watch her break the pipe, so I'd know she meant it. She broke it in half and threw it on the kitchen floor. Then we took turns stompin' on it till there wasn't anything left, and all the time we kept yelling at that crack pipe, and cursing it, and cursing the dope man. My mom swept the pieces up in the dustpan and put it in the garbage. That's probably the best thing that happened to me before I became a teenager.

My neighborhood and my friends . . .

When my mom quit crack for good, we moved to L.A. She said she couldn't stay off crack if we stayed in the old neighborhood. Another new neighborhood. Another new school. More new friends.

My mom and I lived in an apartment over a store in South Central LA. It was a strange neighborhood. During the day, you'd see about a thousand people walking around on the street. A lot of them were USC students walking to and from the campus, which was only a few blocks away down near the old county museums. But you couldn't walk around alone anywhere near my building after dark, not if you were smart. The only time I went out on the street at night was when I was with some of my friends. There was a café down on the corner where we used to hang out.

There were about ten of us who hung together a lot. We called ourselves a gang, and we were, in a way. But we weren't like any of the big gangs, nothing like the Bloods or the Crips. We didn't have colors or anything. We weren't like that kind of gang. We weren't organized, didn't even have a bad-ass sounding name. We called ourselves the Jefferson and Hoover gang, because we were all from that neighborhood. We hung together for protection, at school mostly and sometimes on the streets in the neighborhood. I still hang with one of my friends from high school, b'cuz he goes to my college. I see my other old friends once in a while, when I happen to be back in the old neighborhood visiting my mom. But I live in a rooming house now, right near my campus, so mostly I hang with my college friends. I feel sorry for anybody who belongs to a real gang, one of the big, real violent gangs that have all kinds of rules and are into making and dealing drugs. Those kind of gangs are hard to get out of once you're in. If you're in that kind of gang and want to get out, go to a counselor and get some advice.

All my friends were like me. Poor, most of them on welfare. Their mothers were divorced, their fathers far away. The divorce rate in California is 90%, so what do you expect? One of my friend's mom was a crackhead like my mom used to be. A couple of my friends were a year behind in school, but one of them was really smart and got sent ahead a grade.

One of the things we all had in common, that stands out most, was anger. All my friends were angry, every one of them. They should all have been in anger management. One of my old friends, I'll call him Benny, didn't get to finish high school. He was one of the 50%. He dropped out in the ninth grade. He didn't want to take a minimum wage job at McDonald's. Decided to deal dope instead. About a month ago he ended up face down on the sand on Santa Monica Beach, with so many bullet holes in him the cops couldn't count them all. I went to his funeral. Besides me, there were about a dozen people there. His mom, his kid sister, a couple friends from the neighborhood. And two undercover cops. It was a real sad affair.

My school…

I went to a big city middle school in South Central L.A. where the dropout rate was 50%. I'd missed a grade back in Oakland, so I was a grade behind and already fourteen when I entered 7th grade. There were a thousand kids in my school, one of the biggest schools in L.A. Forty kids to a classroom. I don't think that was even legal. My mom said thirty-five was the legal limit, or something like that. The school just wasn't big enough. There were all kinds of kids in my school. There were white kids, black kids, Asian kids, Hispanic kids, Arab American kids, Native American kids. There were kids of every race and every ethnic group and every religion at my school.

When I was still living in Minnesota, I got to go to karate school. I was only ten, but by the time my mom and I moved to Southern California I already knew some katas. A kata is a series of karate moves. The more katas you know, the better. When we moved to L.A., my mom found funds for kids like me whose moms didn't have much income, and so I got to go to a good karate school. I have to tell you, karate school really helped me out a lot, and in a lot of ways. I was small for my age, had always been one of the smallest kids in my age group. I got picked on a lot. After a couple more years of karate with my new sensei, that changed. I didn't get picked on as much anymore. The reason was mostly because I'd gained some self-confidence. It wasn't because I used my karate skills as weapons.

My sensei, that's the head guy in a karate school, the one who knows the most katas, set me straight right from the start. Sensei was a Nisi, a Japanese American. He owned the karate school I went to in Little Tokyo, an area in downtown L.A. where many Japanese Americans still live. Sensei was small like me, but when I saw him break a brick one day with his bare hand and a board with his bare foot, I knew he had some skills that I had to respect. Sensei told me karate was not to be used to hurt others. He said karate was a sacred art form, as well as a system of self-defense. He said people who used karate for anything but self-defense brought dishonor to the art and shame upon the sensei. He said if I ever used karate that way, he'd kick me out of class. I can proudly say I never did use karate to hurt anybody, though I came real close one time. You'll read about that later in my story. Instead, I got real good at hurting people with words. For hurting people, angry words became my best weapons. You could say, I knew a lot of word katas.

My first anger high...

I think I had my first anger high when I was fourteen, when my mom and I came to L.A. It was my first semester at my new school. I was in gym class. I'd showered and was walking back to my locker when I saw the kid whose locker was next to mine open my locker and look inside. I yelled, *"Hey!"* He turned around. I walked up to him, got right in his face, and yelled, *"What the hell are you doing in my locker?"* He looked real indignant. He was wearing glasses that were all steamed up. He took them off and rubbed the steam off them with his finger, crammed them back on his face. He yelled back, *"It's my locker, dude!"* He turned and shut the locker door and pointed at the number. He saw right away that he was wrong. It was my locker, not his. He looked at me again, opened his mouth to say something. I gave him a shove with the palm of my hand, not a hard shove but enough to throw him off balance. He said, *"Hey, watch it!"* He took a couple of steps back, made a fist. I spun around, threw a hard kick at his locker, which was to the left of mine. My bare foot flew past, about an inch from his face. The heel of my foot made a loud crash when it hit. The kid's face got white. *"Okay, okay!"* he said. *"I'm sorry."* I looked at him, drilled his eyes with mine. And, yep, I felt high. I didn't say I'd accepted his apology. I wouldn't even give the dude the satisfaction.

Other kids in the locker room had been watching the action. They didn't say anything, but I knew they'd liked what I did. One of my friends that I hung with a lot was grinning at me, and nodding his head. It meant, you did good, Sean. You showed him!

My mind was already judging the situation and how I acted. I heard Sensei's voice. *"If I ever hear you have hurt anybody with what I have taught you, you will be kicked out of my class. And you will never get back in my class, never."* Well, I said to myself, I didn't hurt the dude, just scared him a little. Sensei never said it was wrong to use karate to scare somebody. No, Sensei never said that. Besides, the kid had it comin'! He broke into my locker! Well, not exactly. I hadn't locked it. I rationalized, I blamed, I minimized.

Looking back, I have to say I was wrong, definitely wrong. I should've handled the situation differently. I hurt that dude's pride. He'd made a mistake about the locker numbers. I knew it was a mistake as soon as I saw his steamed up glasses. I used the situation as an excuse to use anger and my karate skills to intimidate the dude and make him feel small and embarrassed. It wasn't right.

My first consequences . . .

My first consequence happened as a result of my first anger high. When I threw the karate kick at the locker, the gym teacher heard the crash and came running to see what had happened. He saw the dent in the locker door, saw me and the other kid standing there. "*Who did that?*" the gym teacher yelled. He had a temper too. I didn't say anything. Neither did the other kid. He didn't have to. The gym teacher saw the smirk on my face. He marched me down to the Assistant Principal's office, told him what I'd done.

All I got was a warning. When I came out of the office, my friend who'd seen the action in the locker room was waiting in the hall. He gave me high fives, told me how cool it looked when I landed the kick. I don't count that one as a serious consequence. It was more like a reward. Getting sent to the Assistant Principal's office was no big deal. My friend made me feel good about what I'd done, instead of bad. So it was one of those consequences that reinforced my angry behavior. I had a lot of those kinds of consequences.

Later that year, I got in trouble in math class. I hated math. I was never any good at it. I was strictly verbal. I liked to read, I liked to write. I'd kept a journal since I was about ten years old. My best subject had always been English, my worst was math. Anyway, it made me feel real stupid not to be able to do math problems that the other kids could do easily. On this particular day, the teacher wrote two algebra problems on the board. The teacher made me and another kid go up and work on the problems in front of the class, as a kind of race. They were simple algebra problems, but algebra was really hard for me. I could do decimals, could even add and subtract them in my head sometimes. But algebra—forget it. Well, the other kid and I went up to the board. The other kid went right to work solving his problem. I stood there with my back to the class, my mind a blank. I picked up the chalk, then I started to sweat. I had no idea what to do. I felt totally stupid, totally powerless. Finally I slammed the chalk on the floor by my feet, turned around and stomped down the aisle between the seats to the door. Before I got to the door I gave a chair a kick that sent it skidding across the floor into the wall at the back of the room. I threw open the door and ran out into the hall, slamming the door behind me. The teacher ran out behind me and followed me down the hall. She caught up with me just as I got to the exit door. I ended up at the Assistant Principal's office again. This time I wound up in school detention for four weeks—four! That was a bad consequence.

But here's the worst thing that ever happened to me because of my anger. It's my worst consequence. About six months after I scared the kid who opened my locker by mistake, I got in trouble in gym class again. It was at the end of the Spring semester. I got in a yelling match with a kid. It was over something real stupid. I can't even remember what it was about. Like I said, I'm no big dude. I'm nineteen now, and I'm 5'8" and 'bout 150 pounds. I was only fourteen at the time of the shouting match, and was still only 5'5" and weighed maybe 120. But could I yell! I think I got that from my dad. He had a voice like a Marine Corps drill sergeant, deep and loud. I mean, he could rattle the windows. Back then mine wasn't quite as deep but it was plenty loud. Anyway, the gym teacher came running out of his office to see who was gettin' killed. He sees me standing there, with my face about half an inch from the other kid's face. The gym teacher says, *"Oh, you again, huh, Sean?"* Well, first he yells, *"Shut up!,"* then he says, *"You again,"* to me. He tells the other kid to hit the showers. Then he tells me to get my butt to the Assistant Principal's office. I shout an obscenity and head out the exit door into the teachers' parking lot. My adrenaline was really pumpin'. I was so angry! I was walking up and down between the rows of cars. I wasn't looking for it, but I saw the gym teacher's car parked in a slot near the exit I'd just run out of. His car was maybe a year old at the most. I'd seen him driving it a few times over the year, so I knew it was his car all right. I stopped in front of the car. I looked at it, and I swear I could see the gym teacher's face in the headlamps. I had on my gym shoes. Well, you can probably guess what I did. Right, I threw some karate kicks and broke out the headlamps. Then I ran around to the back of the car, and kicked out the taillights. He was watching from the door.

Bet you can guess what happened next. Yep, the cops came and hauled me away. By four o'clock, I was in a Detention Center lockup. I got expelled from school for the rest of the year. The following September they sent me to an alternative high school, a school for troublemakers like me. The teachers were tough. They had to be. They were trying to deal with 30 teenagers, all of them full of anger, most of them on probation. The teachers were tough, yes, but they also cared. The teachers at my old school cared too, don't get me wrong. They just didn't know how to handle angry kids like me. And with 40 kids in the classroom, they had other things to do besides try to keep order. Teachers like to teach. They don't like trying to be cops. It's not their job.

I did good in alternative school. I got counseling while I was there too. We all did. Of course, being on probation I didn't have a choice about that. It was one of the conditions of probation. I had to go and see the school counselor once a week whether I needed it or not. Usually, I needed it. The counselor helped me more than I sometimes like to admit. She helped me to see that I had some good stuff inside me, that I should try to bring out.

How I learned my angry behavior

I wasn't born with an anger problem. Nobody is. I learned my anger problem. Somewhere along the way, my anger got out of control. It became a pattern, a habit. I used anger more and more to deal with the world. I began abusing anger. The more I used anger, the more I wanted to use it. The more I used it, the more I forgot how to use other ways to get my needs met. My anger got out of control. I learned a lot of my anger from the kids I hung out with. It seemed like all my friends were angry. I learned part of my anger from my mom. It seemed like my mom was angry all the time. My mom's anger was always worse when her supply of crack cocaine ran out. Anyway, I saw my mom acting angry, saw how she did it, the kinds of things she did, heard the words she used, and how she used her voice. I ended up with an anger habit a lot like hers. I guess it's a pretty common anger pattern. She yelled—loud! I learned to yell loud too. Sometimes when she'd get mad, she'd run at me shaking her fists. Sometimes she swore. She never beat me up, not even when I was little. But she threatened to. After she'd get angry, sometimes she'd kick back in a chair or lie on the couch and look very relaxed. I'd even see her smiling sometimes.

One time I saw my mom get angry at the welfare office, and we ended up getting a few more food stamps that month. I saw that she got what she wanted by using anger. She got good results. Anyway, I learned how to act angry by watching and listening to my mom. My dad used to get angry too, usually when he was drunk. I learned some of my anger from him, but I learned most of my anger from my mom.

I wasn't aware I was learning how to be angry by watching my mom's angry behavior. And she wasn't aware she was my main anger teacher. It seemed like some part of my mind was learning the angry behavior without me knowing it. In fact, now I know that's how it works. A part of the mind I wasn't even aware of was doing the learning. Counselors call it the *unconscious* part of the mind. It's the same part we use in order to learn how to walk and talk. It seems like it just happens. Think back over your life and see if you learned your anger habit the way I learned mine.

And by the way, you aren't "sick." Don't let anybody tell you that's why you have an anger problem. You're not crazy or stupid either. You have an anger problem, and you're the one responsible. Sorry, but it's true. When I found that out, I didn't like it either. I'd rather have blamed somebody, like my mom or some of the other people in my life.

I used to watch a lot of violent programs on television. Used to play violent video games. TV and video games were some of my other anger teachers. I couldn't stop hanging out with my mom, but I could stop watching TV and stop playing violent video games. And I did. I've got other things to do with my time now.

CHAPTER TWO

Sean's Recovery Story

My Recovery from My Anger Habit

To begin with, I'm not recovered. I'm in recovery. That means I still have an anger problem but I've changed my worst angry behavior and am learning how to change the other parts of my whole self, so that I can learn how to live a contented rage-free life, not just avoid consequences. You'll learn more about the whole self later in the book. Don't worry. Don't rush it.

After I got out of the Detention Center, I was on probation. Being on probation involves a lot of rules. They call them conditions. I'm telling you, if you're not already on probation, change your behavior real fast. You don't want to end up on probation, like I was. The probation officers, not your mom or dad, make all the rules. They tell you how late you can stay out, who you can hang out with, where you can hang out. They tell you where you can work. And they make other rules you have follow too. There are other conditions you have to satisfy. And if you don't follow them, you get violated. That means you get some kind of a consequence. The kind of consequence depends on which rule or condition you break. You might get yelled at. You might get a year added on your probation time. You might get sent back to the Detention Center. If you're over sixteen, you might go to the county jail. You could even end up in prison.

Anyway, one of my rules of probation was I couldn't use alcohol or other drugs. My probation officer said if I was caught using any non-prescribed drug even once, even alcohol, he'd send me to drug and alcohol counseling. Well, that's what happened. If you're on probation, they check your urine. They do it randomly, which means you never know when they're going to check. I thought I had it all figured out, thought I recognized a pattern of when they were most likely to check. It looked like they were most likely to check on Mondays. So I sneaked about three hits on a blunt one Tuesday night. Wouldn't you know it? My probation officer calls the next day and tells me to report that afternoon for a urine test. I took some over-the-counter stuff a friend of mine said would cancel out the m.j. It didn't. Sure enough, they found marijuana in my urine. It wasn't a very high reading, but enough to show. Bam!—I had to go to D & A counseling. Another time I got tested, it showed Robitussin. My probation officer said if they found any kind of drug in my urine again—anything at all—even the tiniest bit of alcohol, while I was still on probation, he'd violate me and I'd go back to the Detention Center till I was eighteen. Believe me, I stopped using marijuana. I stopped using alcohol—I stopped using anything! For a while, I was even afraid to take an aspirin. Actually, for me it wasn't a big deal. I wasn't into drugs and alcohol like a lot of my friends were. I'd use whatever was around, if I didn't have to pay for it. And I did get to liking a Robo trip once in a while. I was also afraid all the time that Sensei would find out. Sensei would kick anybody out of class if he knew you'd been using any kind of drug. He said using drugs was stupid, sort of like dumping glue into a Rolex watch.

I said a lot of my friends, in fact all of my friends, back in the old neighborhood had a problem with anger. So I stopped hanging out with them, even the ones who weren't on my no-see list because I knew I'd end up acting the same old way again if I didn't stay away from them. That wasn't easy, I mean to just break old friendships. But it's what I had to do. One of them, the dude that quit school and started selling drugs, was on my probation officer's list anyway. If I hung out with anybody who was known to be selling drugs, I'd get violated. So I stopped hanging with my dope dealer friend, no trouble. But my other friends, the ones my probation officer hadn't put on my no-see list, were harder to let go of. But I did. And you know what? I didn't miss them all that much. They didn't seem to miss me either.

Another one of my conditions was I had to go to anger management. That really made me mad! Just kidding. No, that's a lie. Getting sent to anger management did make me mad. I was already going once a week to drug and alcohol counseling, and two AA meetings as well. I was working my butt off at school trying to get my grades up, so I could get my high school diploma, another condition of probation. And I had to attend anger management on top of all that. It seemed like I didn't have a minute to myself—damn! Anyway, my probation officer sentenced me to Pathways to Peace. I knew I'd done stuff that wasn't right. I'd damaged school property, did about $1,000 worth of damage to the gym teacher's car. Scared my teachers. But I didn't really think I had an anger problem. I was in denial about that. Maybe most of my friends needed anger management, but not me.

My probation officer said I had to go to at least sixteen Pathways to Peace meetings, and if I missed any meetings—the reason didn't matter—I had to make them up. I had to be appropriate while in group, which meant I'd better not do any of my angry behaviors. No yelling, no intimidating anybody. Those were the basic rules. They were the same as the Pathways to Peace rules, now that I think about it. But on top of all that, my probation officer said I had to participate. I said, what does that mean? He said I had to attend meetings regularly. I had to read from the book when asked. I had to answer questions if the group leader asked me any, and I had to keep up with the written work. So I went to my meetings, missing only one out of sixteen groups and which I made up. I read from the book. I nodded yes or no if the group leader asked me a question. I scribbled down some answers to the self-tests. But that's all I did—the bare minimum. Just enough to satisfy the conditions of probation. In other words, all I did was comply.

I'm still going to my group, by the way. I started when I was fourteen. I'm nineteen now so I've been going to Pathways to Peace for five years. Wait a minute, don't get too bent out of shape. With perfect attendance, you can finish up in sixteen weeks and walk away with a certificate of completion. That is, if you finish the workbook. I don't mean just read the book. You have to finish all the self-tests too. Flip through a couple chapters. You'll see what I mean. But don't let that worry you either. You don't have to fill in every blank space. A few words, or a phrase or two, is usually all you have to put down. Like I said, I complied.

I finished the book. I got my certificate. I'd complied. I could have stopped going to PTP meetings right then. But I kept going. Well, you could ask, why am I still going to those Pathways to Peace meetings? Because I needed to keep going. Yep, I surprised everybody, including my probation officer. I surprised myself most of all. For once, I was thinking about my future. I still wasn't sure what I wanted to do with my life, but I'd learned enough by going to Pathways to Peace to know that my anger problem was the one thing that would wreck whatever future I decided on. Anyway, I kept going to PTP meetings.

The first thing I was asked to do was complete Chapters 1, 2, and 3, including writing my story. The group leader said I didn't have to write my whole story yet, just sketch in the basic information. He said that would prepare me to complete an honest self-assessment. I read the material and learned what was meant by an honest self-assessment. Thinking back, I knew in my gut there was plenty of evidence to convince anybody else that I had an anger problem. But up till then, there wasn't enough evidence to convince me. A lot of people had told me I had a serious problem with anger. My friends said I had a problem. Coming from them, that was pretty strong evidence, because they had anger problems too. My teachers said so too. So did the police, so did judges, so did my probation officer. Even my mom said I had a problem with anger. But I needed to find it out for myself. It was the only way to break down my wall of denial. And, believe me, I'd built one as thick as the wall that circles Alcatraz.

Of course, I went at it backwards at first. I went right to the self-test at the end of the chapter and circled "no" to almost all of the questions. I made sure I circled "no" to all the questions marked with a star, or asterisk, because the instructions said that a "yes" answer to even one of them shows a serious problem with anger. I thought, for sure, I was being honest when I answered "no" to the first three starred questions. I'd never hurt anybody on purpose because of my anger, not physically anyway. I'd never harmed a family member either, and I sure never harmed myself. People who did that—you know, teens who cut themselves with razor blades—are mental, right? And I sure didn't see myself as one of those. But read on, and you'll see why I had to change my ideas about that too.

Then I made a stupid mistake, at least I thought so at the time. I asked the group leader to explain about question number one on the self-test. Question number one had a star and said, *"Have you ever harmed anyone because of your anger?"* I asked the group leader if the question meant, have you ever done physical harm to anyone. He said, yes, it meant that. Then he said the question also meant, have you ever harmed anybody's feelings because of your anger? Have you ever made somebody feel scared, or made them feel stupid—stuff like that? Oh, oh, I said to myself. I'd done that plenty of times. I'd hurt a lot of people's feelings when I got angry, including my mother. That meant I had to circle "yes" to both of the first two questions, and they both had stars. That made me think a little more honestly about question number three, *"Have you ever harmed yourself when angry?"* Well, I never cut myself, never beat on myself with a stick or something. Then I looked down at the little finger on my right hand, the finger with the first joint that was all crooked and bent, and always would be. When I was only about eight years old, I got really angry at my mother one day. I don't remember why. Anyway, I went in my room and punched the wall real hard. It made me feel real powerful to do that, especially when I saw the dents my fist put in the wallboard. It hurt my fist a little, but not much. I punched the wall three times. But I didn't know about how walls were made, that about every sixteen inches or so there was a two-by-four stud. The third time I slugged the wall, I hit one of those studs. Result? Broken finger. Pain. So I had hurt myself that time because of anger. In fact there were other times when I punched a wall and hurt my hand. Nothing broken, but one time I sprained my wrist real bad. Anyway, if I was going to be honest, I had to answer "yes" to question number three. By the time I got to question number six, my denial was pretty well shot. And question number seven? I mean, how could I deny that I got arrested for something, where anger was a factor?

I went ahead and scribbled down some of my personal story, then took another look at the self-assessment. There was no way I could honestly circle "no" to any of the questions. My self-assessment showed I had a problem with anger all right, and it was a serious problem. One thing I liked about the self-assessment was it was my assessment not somebody else's. Some authority figure I resented didn't do the assessment, I did. What I didn't like about the self-assessment was, since I was the one who read the questions and circled the answers and scored the results, then I had to own the results. I admitted to a serious problem with anger. I admitted I'd harmed other people. I hadn't hurt anybody physically but I'd definitely hurt people's feelings, and I'd scared people. I admitted I'd damaged property, and I admitted I'd harmed myself. I did something to somebody's property and ended up in the Detention Center, and robbed myself of my freedom. I got kicked out of school and got put on probation, and had to go to an alternative school. Anyway, I couldn't deny the problem anymore. The wall of denial I'd built came crashing down around my ears. I ended up answering "yes" to every single question on that stupid self-assessment! Next, I read and signed the Anti-Violence Self-Agreement.

At first I only admitted these things to myself. The Pathways to Peace group leader told me it would help a lot if I also admitted all these things to somebody else. He said I should ask whoever I chose to witness the agreement by signing it too. The group leader told me to make sure the person I chose would understand, and not judge me too much. I'd made friends with a teen in my group who'd been in the Pathways to Peace program for a couple of years, a seventeen-year-old kid who sort of became my PTP sponsor. I'll call him Jack. A couple of months after I did my self-assessment, I had a talk with Jack about it. He listened to me, asked if I was really serious about the whole thing or was I just trying to satisfy a condition of probation. I told Jack I was serious. I was, too. He said okay, and signed where it said witness. So having completed the self-agreement, I had begun the first of the eight-step process suggested by Pathways to Peace as a way to stop my angry behavior. **Step One** is the *Admission Step*. It says *"Admit you caused harm. Apologize and make restitution."* I'd admitted I'd caused harm and, so, acknowledged that I had a problem with anger. But I still hadn't done anything about the second part of the step.

Next, I made some apologies. I got permission from my probation officer to go and meet with the principal of my old school, the one I'd been kicked out of because of my angry behavior. I'd damaged school property when I threw the karate kick at the locker. I'd thrown a scare into the kid I thought had got into my locker on purpose. Now that some time had passed, I found myself feeling guilty—who woulda thought? Anyway, I made an appointment to meet with the principal. I also said I'd like to meet with the kid I scared, at the same time I met with the principal. It was all arranged just like I wanted it. The principal accepted my apology and shook hands with me. Believe it or not, it made me feel good. But it was different with the kid I'd scared when I grazed his cheek with the karate kick. He listened to my apology. When I was done, he looked at me. He squinted his eyes almost shut, and called me a name I can't write down. I didn't expect that. I thought the kid would've accepted my apology like the principal had. Nope. It made me feel real embarrassed. I felt my gut get real tight, which is what happens to me when an anger trigger happens. I caught myself, somehow. I didn't attack back, with words. I didn't go into my karate intimidation act. I took a deep breath and forced myself to relax my posture. That gave me time to think. I remembered what the Pathways to Peace group leader had said when I told him about the meeting I was going to have at my old school. He'd said, *"Be sure and remember this, Sean: the apologies you're going to make are for your benefit, not their's."* Then he said, *"If it happens to make them feel good too, that's okay."* About a week later, I got permission to meet with the gym teacher. I owed him an apology, that's for sure. I put his car off the road for about a week. I met with him in his office. The Assistant Principal was there too. The gym teacher knew I was going to Pathways to Peace, and he knew about how the program worked. So after I'd apologized, he asked me if I had a job. I said, no. Then he said, *"Well how're you going to make restitution?"* I didn't know what to say. He said, *"How're you going to pay me back for what it cost to have my car fixed?"* I said, *"Well, didn't your insurance pay for it?"* He said, *"Sure, about half of it."* The repair bill was $1,000. The gym teacher had to pay the first $500 out of his pocket. I began to feel real powerless. I was going to school full time and my probation officer had me going to so many programs after school, there was no way I could squeeze a part-time job into my schedule—no way. The gym teacher watched me struggle with my thoughts. I know my face was turning red. Finally, he said, *"How about washing my car?"* I said, *"How many times?"* He said, *"Ten times."* I said, *"It's a deal."* He said, *"You're getting off easy."* I said, *"I know."* Anyway, I ended up making restitution by washing the gym teacher's car ten times. I made restitution.

But I couldn't always apologize to people I'd hurt or repay people whose property I'd damaged. Some people I had hurt had moved away. I didn't have their addresses, so I had no way of reaching them. In one instance, I managed to get the address of a kid I'd embarrassed real bad one time when I was in 6th grade. Later, the kid went to live with his dad. But I knew where his mother lived, and so I went and got his new address from her. Guess who I apologized to last? Yep, my mom. It's harder to work the Pathways to Peace program with your family than with people outside your family. You'll see.

I made apologies and restitution in order to get rid of the guilt and shame. I had a lot of guilt and shame, even if I wasn't always aware of it. And I knew guilt and shame stood in my way. I had to deal with it. So I made apologies and restitution. It helped put the guilt and shame behind me. I was only fourteen when I did Step One the first time. But I've had to take the Admission Step more than once, especially the second part. I stopped damaging other people's property, but every now and then I'd get angry and damage something of my own, or I'd end up saying or doing something that hurt somebody's feelings. About a year ago, I got mad at my mom about something and threw my MP3 player against the wall. She's the one who bought it for me. Of course, she got mad at me for throwing it. And it made her feel bad too, because it had cost her over $100 and had been a special Christmas gift to me. Anyhow, I damaged it. Lucky for me, the MP3 player still works, but it won't display correctly anymore. So if I happen to get it wet, if it gets rained on or something, my expensive MP3 player will be history. After I damaged it, I had to admit to myself I still had a problem with anger. About a week later, I apologized to my mom. She accepted my apology. Moms—what makes them that way? No matter what, they almost always forgive you.

Next, I moved on to **Step Two:** *Take Responsibility*. This step says, *"Take responsibility for your actions, decide to stop your harmful behavior, and become willing to forgive yourself and others."* I'd already started taking responsibility for my behavior when I took Step One. And I'd decided to stop my harmful behavior. The last part of Step Two, "…become willing to forgive others and yourself," was the hard part. It's still the hardest part. In the past, I always blamed others. I wouldn't own my behavior, and I wouldn't own the consequences. Blaming others had always been part of my denial. It was the mortar that held the wall together. Finally, I saw I would have to own my behavior, and I would have to own the results of my behavior.

I also saw I had to become willing, at least, to forgive those who harmed me. There was my father who left me, and my mother who took me away from my father and wouldn't tell me where he was. I knew I'd also have to become willing to forgive myself for what I'd done to others. I could see by now that willingness to forgive was real important. The Pathways to Peace program told me the act of forgiving would free me up from guilt and shame and help me get rid of my resentment. I knew these things kept me stuck. I was ready to become willing to forgive others and myself, but I sure wasn't ready to actually do it. The chapter on Forgiveness is way at the back of the book. I can see why. So will you, if you don't already.

The next step in my recovery, Step Three, wasn't easy either. **Step Three** told me I had to *"Realize you are never justified in using violence."*

My self-assessment made me confront my beliefs about violence. I used to believe violence was justified—often. C'mon now! You could take just so much, right? What if you tried to reason with people, and they just wouldn't listen? What if people just laughed in your face? What if you compromised, and people took advantage of you? Wasn't violence justified then? And there was the war on terror, the war on drugs. And there was the war against Adolph Hitler, who wanted to take over the world and make everybody do the goose step. Wasn't violence justified in those situations?

The Pathways to Peace group leader helped me see this step differently. He said I wasn't asking the questions in the right way. I was asking about violence in a general way. I needed to ask myself about violence in a personal way. First I needed to make a self-statement based on my self-assessment. I needed to say, *"Sean, you have a problem with anger. You get drunk on anger and rage. When you get angry, you harm others. Then you pay dues—as a result of your anger, you lose things."* So I turned the issue of violence into a personal issue. Then I asked myself a personal question. *"Sean,"* I said, *"as a person with a serious anger problem, can I ever justify using angry, violent behavior?"* Finally I stopped arguing with myself, or with anybody else. Maybe some people think violence is justified. Maybe they can afford to think so. But I couldn't, not as a person with an anger problem. No, I'd already paid enough dues. So I decided to hold a new belief about violence. I now believe that, for me, violence in any form is never justified. Believing violence is never justified, I'm a lot less likely to use violent words or actions when a bad feeling triggers my anger.

Now I was ready to take a look at Step Four of the recovery process. **Step Four** said, *"Learn new ways to feel personal power without violating other people's right to feel safe in their person and property."* I'd learned early on that anger made me feel powerful. I learned that in the locker room when I karate-kicked the locker door and scared the kid with the glasses, and copped my first anger high. I'd learned to use anger to feel powerful whenever I felt powerless, and when I used anger I ended up hurting other people or their property, and hurting myself. Then I ended up with consequences. I lost things, like my freedom. By then I knew I'd have to find new ways to feel powerful. I'd have to learn some skills to deal with anger triggers. Then I started making a serious effort to learn new ways to feel powerful that didn't violate other people's right to feel safe.

Once I learned some skills to help myself stop using angry words and actions, I could go on to Step Five. **Step Five** asked me to *"treat people and property with respect and dignity, the respect and dignity that I, too, deserve and expect."* Other people had harmed me in the past. They'd hurt me, sometimes really bad. The worst was the dude that molested me. He'd hurt me about every way anybody could be hurt. He made me feel worthless. I'm still getting over what he did to me, slowly but surely! But I began to see that I was passing on the pain I'd suffered to others. I'd used anger and rage to make other people feel worthless. I took away their dignity and self-respect. But now I knew the people I'd hurt didn't deserve the pain I caused them, any more than I'd deserved the pain I'd gone through. When I saw that, it made me want to change. I promised myself, that from now on I'd try hard to treat others with dignity and respect, no matter what others had done to me in the past. No matter how others had hurt me. It was a hard promise to keep, and still is. I still put a lot of hard work into this step. Sometimes I still screw up and treat people kind of bad, but not like I used to, and I can usually apologize pretty fast.

It was a lot harder to do what **Step Six**: *Change Negative Beliefs to Positive Beliefs* asked me to do. It was a lot harder than learning new skills. I learned I had a lot of negative beliefs, and learned how they'd kept me stuck in anger and rage. So I took a good look at my beliefs. I learned to identify the ones that kept me stuck, and learned how to let go of them. Then I learned new positive beliefs that would support my recovery. The new beliefs helped me change my angry behavior, and gave me a different outlook on things. Before, I thought I couldn't change. Maybe I thought I wasn't smart enough, or maybe I didn't think I could learn the skills it would take to change my angry behavior. Anyhow I believed I couldn't change, and that negative belief kept me stuck in anger. If I can't change, I said to myself, then why should I try? After reading more of the guidebook, I decided I could change after all, if I decided to believe I could. By then I'd learned some new skills to help myself change, and I'd found out the skills worked, so it wasn't too hard to adopt the new belief that I could change.

Step Seven: *Find Your Purpose* was hard. The step asked me to come to believe I could change and that I had some special purpose to fulfill. The first part wasn't too hard, actually. I'd already learned I could change, and had come to believe that I could. But the second part, which asked me to believe that I had some special purpose to fulfill, wasn't so easy. I struggled with that part.

When I first started reading the Pathways to Peace literature and attending Pathways to Peace meetings, I thought I had no reason to change. No reason, that is, other than to avoid getting violated by breaking my conditions of probation. I thought I might be able to stop my angry behavior using the skills I'd learned at least until I got off probation, and then maybe I could avoid going back to the Detention Center. In other words, I thought I could change my behavior temporarily in order to avoid consequences. But I didn't think I had any reason other than that to change.

Before working Step Seven, I actually thought my life had no special purpose, no special meaning. I couldn't see any special purpose to my life or to anyone else's life. We're born, we live, then we die—that was it. That was another belief that kept me stuck, that life had no special meaning. If life had no special meaning, I asked myself, then why should I change? I mean, why should I change my angry behavior once I'm off probation? I could see that if I didn't, I'd probably end up back on probation again. Or worse, maybe I'd end up in jail or prison. If my life doesn't have any special reason, and nobody else's does either, then why should I change? Why should anybody change? Why should I stop using anger to feel powerful? Why should I try to treat other people with respect and dignity, especially if it really didn't matter in the long run? Well, I tried to work the step anyway, even though, at first, I couldn't make any sense out of it.

I ended up asking myself a lot of what I thought were dumb questions. Remember, I already believed my life had no special meaning, no purpose. So when I asked myself, *"Why am I on the earth?"* or *"What is my special purpose?,"* the questions sounded real stupid. Soon as I asked the questions, my brain said, *"Those are stupid questions! You already believe there's no special reason for being alive."* So I had to ask myself a different question. I said, *"If I had some special reason for being alive, what could it be?"* The part of me that thought all such questions were stupid kept shouting, *"There is no reason, stupid!"* *"Shut up!"* I told that part, *"I'm the one who decides what I'm going to believe, not you."* The part of my brain that believed my life and nobody else's had any meaning finally did shut up. Then I started to get different answers. You'll find out exactly what I came to believe, later in the workbook. Anyway, it took a while, but I finally learned I not only had the ability to change, I found out that my life did have a special purpose. So now I had hope. I had a reason to change my angry behavior that was big enough to get me through times when everything seemed all wrong and nothing made sense. What made me change my beliefs about my life? I found out I couldn't change my angry behavior and avoid worse consequences than I'd already had, if I still got up every morning saying to myself, *"Life sucks, and then you die."* In order to come to believe my life had some kind of special purpose, I also had to change my attitude and my outlook. That meant, I finally understood, that I had to change my spiritual beliefs.

I worked hard at changing my behavior, and just as hard at changing my character. I worked the Pathways to Peace program as hard as I could. Basic changes started to happen, positive changes. Not only did my behavior change, my attitude changed. My outlook changed—my character changed. **Step Eight**: *Transformation* started to happen, almost as though on its own. I began to be transformed. But that doesn't mean I'm done. It doesn't mean I'm done changing. Or done growing. Step Eight says, *"Continue working your anger management program. Continue to grow and change. Forgive others and yourself, and help other angry people find their Pathway to Peace."*

I forgave those who had harmed me. I forgave myself for the harm I'd done. I committed myself to helping others recover from their anger problem. That's part of my life purpose. I continue my personal program of emotional, mental, and spiritual growth. I wrote my story about my anger and about my life before coming to PTP. Then I told my story to somebody else. I needed to share it, in order to fully recover. Then I wrote about my recovery. I knew this could help other angry people recover.

Other good things were happening in my life, too. I got through high school. Started writing every day. Participated in some poetry slams around L.A. and found out people liked my stuff, especially my raps. I entered a teenage rap contest and won first prize! Man, did that make me feel good! It was a new way to feel good about myself, a new way to feel like my life had some special purpose after all.

Don't get me wrong, okay? I'm not trying to make you think I didn't have a hard time working the Pathways to Peace recovery steps. It was hard. It still is! When I got to Step Seven: *Find Your Purpose*, like I said I really got stuck. But I finally found out what I was living for, and that it connected with my writing. One of the good things that happened while I was locked up at the Detention Center was I started doing some serious writing. I wrote my first rap poem when I was there. I'd listened to a lot of raps, mostly violent stuff with a lotta four letter words. Looking back, I can see the stuff I was listening to really fed my anger.

The first rap I wrote at the Detention Center was a rant. What's a rant? A rant is an angry poem, an angry rap. While writing that first rap, I became aware, kinda suddenly, that my whole life up until then had been a rant. I'd been angry, angry, angry. I was angry at the whole world. I was angry at my parents, at my teachers, at my friends, at myself. I was angry at the government, angry at all governments. I was angry at rich people. When I started writing my story, I could see that I wasn't the only person in my family whose life was a rant. My dad's life was like that too. He'd been angry at the world all his life too. My mom said he wanted me to be born so that he wouldn't get drafted and have to go and kill people in Vietnam, or get killed himself. My mom said my grandpa, on my dad's side, was angry too. He grew up during what they called the Cold War, when the U.S. and the U.S.S.R. were aiming hydrogen bomb missiles at each other, and rich people were building fallout shelters in their basements and were ready to shoot their neighbors, who couldn't afford to build shelters, if they tried to get in. Anyway, my life had been a rant poem. The poem I wrote got snatched by a guard, who showed it to my counselor, who said he thought it was pretty good. My counselor was sort of a rap artist himself, a forty-year-old black guy named Mr. Johnson who grew up in Watts. He read the stuff he wrote to a jazz beat, snapping his fingers to keep the rhythm of the words. He was good! Not only could Mr. Johnson rap, he was also the best counselor at the Detention Center. Mr. Johnson had a master's degree in social work, an MSW. He drove a nice car, had a pretty wife and a couple of kids. But he started out like me and most of the other kids at the Center. He grew up poor, got in trouble in his teens. Then he turned around. I had to go see Mr. Johnson at least once a week for counseling. We made a deal. Every time I went, I had to read him a new rap I'd written, and he'd read one of his new jazz poems. By the time I got out of the Detention Center, I wasn't afraid to read out loud to an audience. I did my first public rap at a coffee shop in Venice Beach. Mr. Johnson was there. Man, did I feel proud!

Sometimes I still get angry. I'm human, not perfect. Sometimes I get a little loud, you know, I yell once in a while. But since I began my recovery I haven't hurt anyone or damaged property—wait a minute, get honest, Sean! I admit I've had a few slips of the tongue. I've called people names that hurt them. But in each case I apologized soon after. No one has had to call the police on me. I haven't spent any more time locked up. Now I have friends who don't have anger problems and don't abuse drugs. I just finished my first semester of college. I have a girlfriend at college who shares my interests and values. I respect others and I respect myself. I still struggle sometimes, and my life isn't always easy. But I work my program hard every day, and I keep improving and growing. I still go to my Pathways to Peace group once a week. I'm even thinking about starting a group on my college campus.

I never thought I'd ever be happy, but I am. Sometimes I find it hard to believe, but I'm happier than I ever imagined I could be. I've found my Pathway to Peace. I've made peace with most of the people who hurt me in the past. I've made peace with myself. I've made peace with the world. I have a clear purpose. It's to stay focused on my recovery from anger and rage, and to use my writing and performing skills to help other people with an anger problem find their pathway to peace. It's my mission.

MY FUTURE

What I want to accomplish . . .

Because of the Pathways to Peace program, I now understand why it's important to think about my future. It's not something I want to just happen. That's the way it used to be, when I was full of anger and doing angry things in order to cop a feeling of power. Then, of course, I ended up with consequences that I didn't want and didn't anticipate. Nope, that's not the way I want it to be anymore. When stuff happens, I want to be the one making the plans. I want to choose my future. I know what my real values are now, and I have goals that'll get me to them.

Of course I want to stay free from anger as much as possible, otherwise I won't accomplish anything—at least not anything worthwhile. I want to keep writing rap poems, but I want to write a book someday, too. I want to write a novel. So, becoming a professional writer is what I want to accomplish most. It all fits into my life purpose, by the way. Yep, I want to be a writer. I want to finish college with a degree in English. That's pretty general, but because it's general it leaves more than one door open. With a major in English, I could throw some other credits with it and get a teaching degree. With a teaching job I could support myself while I write my book. Or I could use my English degree to become a journalist. I could make a living doing that too. Anyhow, becoming a writer and writing a novel are what

I want to accomplish most. And I want to use what I write, whether rap poems or books, to help angry teens change their behavior.

How I want to be remembered . . .

I never spent time thinking about the long-distance future before. But one night at a Pathways to Peace meeting, the topic for discussion was how each of us at the group wanted to be remembered after we died. I thought it was a stupid topic. Only one person in the group was over eighteen, some dude who'd been in the group since he was about ten, I guess. I don't know, maybe he was born in a Pathways to Peace group. I was only sixteen at the time. Being dead wasn't something I thought about. I knew the group leader and he'd helped me out a lot, so I decided to humor him. Anyhow, the group leader asked us all to imagine we had just died. A couple of the people in the group refused. Like me they thought it was stupid. They sat there and rolled their eyes. I kicked back and closed my eyes and imagined I'd died, and all that. People came to my funeral. They filed past my casket and saw me lying there, eyes closed, face all made up, hair all thin and white. I was 'bout ninety years old. While I was imagining all this, I remembered the motivation strategy in Chapter Eight of *The Pathways to Peace Anger Managment Workbook.* I remembered I was asked to imagine what people were saying about me behind my back, so I applied that same idea to the exercise. After giving it some thought, here's what I came up with. Here's how I want to be remembered. I want people to remember me as a good person—yeah, laugh at me if you want. I want to be remembered as a good writer, too, and somebody who could control his anger. I want to be remembered as somebody who'd made a lot of mistakes starting out but made up for it in the end. Most of all, I want to be remembered as somebody who gave a damn.

Mr. Johnson called me up the other day. You remember, my counselor at the Detention Center. He said he wanted me to come back and do some of my raps for the kids at the Detention Center where I used to be. I couldn't believe it! Of course, I said I would. So one of my main goals right now is to get some of my best raps printed in a pamphlet, go and read them to kids at the Detention Center, and then give a copy of my raps to any kid who wants one. Maybe it'll help some kid like me.

By the way, who would've thought? I mean, who would've thought Sean, one of the worst angry kids from South Central, would end up doing something worthwhile for somebody else?

There, I'm done. Whoever you are, I hope you can relate to some of my story. I hope some of it helps you. But if you don't get anything at all out of my story, that's okay. You don't owe me, and I know I did my best.

Peace,

Sean

SELF-TEST

1. In his story, Sean talked about "bad things" that happened to him. Did you have bad things happen to you?

   YES   NO

2. Sean's mom and dad split up when Sean was seven years old. Did your mom and dad split up?

   YES   NO

3. Sean said he got depressed, then angry when his mom and dad split up. If your mom and dad split up, did you feel depressed and angry?

   YES   NO

4. Sean said the worst thing that happened to him was when, at age ten, he was molested. In a few words, describe the worst thing that has happened to you.

5. Sean also listed some good things that happened to him. List some of the good things that have happened to you.

6. Sean said he experienced his first anger high when he was thirteen years old. How old were you when you had your first anger high?

   I was _____ years old when I had my first anger high.

7. Sean had a consequence as a result of his first anger high. Did you experience a consequence as a result of your first anger high?

   YES   NO

8. Sean said the consequence he had was more like a reward than a consequence, because his friends gave him high fives and told him what he had done was cool. Was your first anger consequence more like a reward?

   YES   NO

9. Sean described the worst consequence he had as a result of his angry behavior. In a few words, describe the worst consequence you have had as a result of your angry behavior.

10. Sean said he ended up in a Detention Center because of his angry behavior. Have you ever been in a Detention Center because of angry behavior?

YES   NO

11. In his story Sean described how he learned his anger habit. Write down one or two of the ways you have learned your anger habit.

. . . .

CHAPTER THREE

The Self-Assessment Process

The Importance of Self-Honesty

As you can see from Sean's story, self-honesty is extremely important. It means being true to yourself. You have to be true to yourself right from the start. It is the one requirement in the self-assessment process. You can't lie to yourself.

Watch out for one big trap: denial. **Denial** means that you want to deny that you have a problem with anger at all. Watch out for three smaller traps. They will trip you up and make self-honesty impossible. They will cause you to lie to yourself. Then you will fall into the trap of denial. So watch out for:

1. **Rationalizing:** To rationalize means to make excuses. The following statement is an example of rationalizing:

   He (or she) wouldn't leave me alone. He (or she) just kept at me.
   That's why I screamed at (or hit) him (or her).

That statement might even be true. But when you use statements like that as an excuse to hurt somebody, you have fallen into the trap of rationalizing.

MESSAGE FROM SEAN

Yep, I'm back already. If you think I'm in your face too much, I'm sorry. If some of the things I say make you angry, I don't blame you. Later, I think you'll change your mind about me. You might even get to like me. Anyway, I want to say something here, right now, before you toss this whole book in the garbage. People lie to themselves all the time. I mean, they do things that make them feel dumb or ashamed or guilty—who wants to feel that way, right? Then they make up a lie to explain away the behavior and make themselves feel better. So when I say "don't lie to yourself," I'm not being disrespectful. I mean, take an honest look at your behavior and an honest look at your feelings. That's all. And guess what? I still lie to myself sometimes. But I've learned to catch myself at it, and then kick back and take a more honest look.

Sean

- -

SELF-TEST

Have you ever used rationalizing in order to excuse your angry behavior?

YES   NO

Think of a time at school or at home, or in a social situation when you were out with your friends, when you got angry and used rationalizing to excuse or defend your angry behavior. Write down one or two examples.

- -

2. **Minimizing:** Minimizing means lying to yourself about how angry you get, or lying to yourself about how often you get angry. The following statements are examples of minimizing:

I never get too angry.

I hardly ever get angry.

. . . .

SELF-TEST

Have you ever used minimizing to excuse your anger?

YES   NO

Think of a time at school or at home, or in a social situation when you were out with your friends, when you got angry, then used minimizing to excuse or defend your angry behavior. Write down one or two examples.

. . . .

3. **Blaming:** Blaming means lying to yourself about responsibility. It means telling others it is their fault.

My father used to beat me up when I was a kid. For no reason. It's my father's fault I am so angry now, not my fault.

That's an example of blaming. Even if your father really did beat you up for no reason when you were a kid, if you use it as an excuse for hurting somebody in the present, then you have fallen into the trap called blaming.

. . . .

SELF-TEST

Have you ever used blaming to excuse your anger?"

YES   NO

Think of a time at school or at home, or in a social situation when you were hanging out with your friends, when you got angry, then used blaming to excuse or defend your angry behavior. Write down one or two examples.

. . . .

Write Your Story

Write your story. Use Sean's story as a guide. Tell about your childhood. Tell about how you developed your anger problem. Tell about the things you did when you were angry. Tell about your results. Tell about the consequences you experienced. Finally, tell about how things are now.

A Special Note

In writing your story, never write down anything that would or could hurt or get you in trouble in any way. Also take care not to write down anything that might get someone else, such as a friend or relative, in trouble. Maybe it would be best to only use first names, or even fake names. Don't disclose anything personal that you would not want someone else to read. What if you lose your workbook, or someone steals it? Think of that when you write down your story. Maybe you think you need to write down, for its therapeutic benefit, something personal which is potentially damaging to yourself or others. Maybe you think writing it down will help you get it off your chest, once and for all. In a case like that, write it down on a separate piece of paper. After writing it down and reading it to yourself, tear the paper up and throw it in the garbage.

However, if you have committed a serious criminal offense against another person, then that offense should be addressed. You need to talk about the offense with someone, both for the other person's sake and for your sake. In such a case you should contact a professional counselor. You should talk to a certified social worker, or a licensed clergy person, or some other professional in the counseling field. If they hold a license or credential, then they will have to act according to the laws governing client/counselor confidentiality. They could not legally share information about you with any other person without your written consent. **NOTE:** That doesn't mean that a professional counselor could not share information with the legal system if your case indicated a need for such a disclosure. For example, if you told a professional counselor or clergy person that you had seriously injured someone, or killed someone, or if you said that you planned to injure or kill someone, the counselor would then be obligated by law to report that information to the proper authorities.

Some Important Points to Remember as You Write Your Story

1. Don't worry about spelling. Don't worry about grammar. Don't worry about punctuation. Just get your story down on paper. That's the important thing.

2. Writing your story might, at times, cause you to remember negative events from your past that might lead to negative feelings. If that happens, stop and talk things over with somebody. Talk to a counselor, or talk to a friend. Then finish your story.

MY STORY

First 12 Years

The year I was born and the places I lived during this time frame…

My father and mother, sisters and brothers…

Bad things that happened to me and how they made me feel…

The worst thing that ever happened to me…

Good things that happened and how they made me feel. . .

My Teen Years

My neighborhood…

My friends…

My first anger high…

My first consequence…

How I learned my anger…

My Future

What I want to accomplish…

How I want to be remembered…

Sharing Your Story

You have written your story. Now it is time to tell your story to someone else, and the sooner the better. In fact, do it now. But choose carefully the person you will tell it to. Make sure you choose someone who will take you seriously. Choose someone who will understand what you are trying to do. Choose someone who is not emotionally linked to you. Choose someone who will not judge you. Explain to him or her that telling your story is a major part of your recovery from your anger problem. Explain that he or she need only listen to your story. Explain that you would rather not have him or her comment or give you feedback.

You could tell your story to a professional counselor, especially if your story contains some "shockers." If you are a member of Pathways to Peace, then you might want to read your story to your Pathways to Peace mentor. You might choose a minister or priest. A family member might not be a good choice. Who will you tell your story to?

SELF-TEST

Now you are ready to do your self-test. It will complete your self-assessment. Read and answer the questions. Be as honest as you can.

1. *Have you ever harmed anyone because of anger?

   YES   NO

2. *Have you ever harmed a family member when angry?

   YES   NO

3. *Have you ever harmed yourself when angry?

   YES   NO

4. *Have you ever been kicked out of school because of anger?

   YES   NO

5. Do you often feel guilt or remorse after getting angry?

   YES   NO

6. *Have you ever purposely damaged someone's property when angry?

   YES   NO

7. *Were you ever arrested where anger was a factor?

   YES   NO

8. Do you often feel unable to control your anger?

   YES   NO

9. Has a friend, family member, or teacher said you have a problem with anger?

   YES   NO

10. Has a counselor or therapist said you have a problem with anger?

    YES   NO

A "yes" answer to just one of the ten questions shows a problem with anger. A "yes" answer to any of the questions marked with an asterisk (*) shows a serious problem with anger.

Have you been honest with yourself? Did the test show you have an anger problem? If so, please study the agreement on the next page carefully. You are urged to sign the agreement before going on to Chapter Four. It is an agreement you make with yourself. It is proof of your desire to change. It is a promise to yourself.

Anti-Violence Self-Agreement

Anti-violence means you are against violence. Self-agreement means you make an agreement with yourself.

If you did an honest self-assessment, you know whether or not you have a problem with anger. If your assessment revealed a problem, then you know you need to change your behavior. Are you serious about changing your violent behavior? If you are, consider the 14-point self-agreement that follows. Look it over closely. Think about it. Then decide.

But don't enter this agreement lightly. It is an agreement you make with yourself. If you violate the agreement, you violate yourself. Not someone else.

If you decide to sign this agreement, have it witnessed. Sign it in the presence of someone you like and admire. And have that person sign as witness.

ANTI-VIOLENCE SELF-AGREEMENT

I, _____ _____, enter the following
agreement with myself:

1. *I agree to admit I have a problem with anger.*
2. *I agree to admit I have harmed others, property, or myself.*
3. *I agree to apologize or make restitution, wherever possible, to those I harmed.*
4. *I agree to accept personal responsibility for the results of my actions.*
5. *I agree to decide to stop my harmful behavior.*
6. *I agree to become willing to forgive those who harmed me.*
7. *I agree to become willing to forgive myself for the harm I have done others.*
8. *I agree I have used violence to feel powerful over people, situations, and things.*
9. *I agree my violence has never been justified and will never be justified.*
10. *I agree to learn non-violent ways to experience personal power.*
11. *I agree not to violate other people's right to feel safe in their person and property.*
12. *I agree to treat all people and their property with respect and dignity.*
13. *I agree to let go of old beliefs that have kept me stuck in anger and violence.*
14. *I agree to search for the purpose of my life and to grow toward that purpose.*

Date_____

Signature_____

Witness_____

The agreement you signed is not just words on paper. It is a binding document. It is a pact with yourself. Signing it means you have made a sincere commitment. You agree to fulfill all of the terms.

If you break this agreement, who will know? You will know. The witness you like and admire will know.

CHAPTER FOUR

Understand the Nature of Anger, Rage, and Violence

Normal Anger Versus Problem or Addictive Anger

Normal Anger

All people get angry, but not all people have a serious problem with anger. In fact, most people don't. When they get angry, most people don't end up seriously harming other people. They don't do serious physical or emotional harm. They don't harm animals or property. They don't harm themselves. They don't use anger to gain power and control over others. Most people use anger only once in a while, and they don't end up with negative results because of anger. They don't end up in serious trouble at home or at school because of their anger. They don't end up being arrested and put on probation.

Problem Anger

Some people, including teenagers, have a serious problem with anger. They have developed an anger habit. In some cases, the habit has turned into an addiction to anger. People who have a serious anger problem often do serious physical or emotional harm to other people or to themselves. They are apt to hurt animals and damage property. They use anger as their main tool for power and control. They use anger often, and they have serious personal consequences. Teens who have a serious anger problem may get arrested and put on probation, or may be sent to a teen detention center. They often lose the respect of their family and friends. Some teens who have a serious problem with anger may become victims of other people's anger. Sometimes they are seriously injured, or even killed by other angry teens.

MESSAGE FROM SEAN

Hi. it's me, Sean. I met a kid at one of my first Pathways to Peace meetings. His name was Juan. He grew up in Arizona. He said he also grew up in a home where somebody was angry every day. He said his mom and dad fought all the time. His older brother used to beat him up. Juan said there was always a lot of screaming and yelling. Things got broken, people got punched or slapped. Juan said he thought that's how it was in everybody's house. I could relate to Juan's story. His house sounded like my house. He thought his was normal. I thought mine was too.

Sean

· ·

SELF-TEST

1. According to the text, not all people have a problem with anger.

   YES   NO

2. According to the text, people who do have a serious problem with anger are apt to hurt other people, animals, and themselves. They are apt to damage property, and they often suffer serious personal consequences.

   YES   NO

· ·

What is Violence?

Visualize a line stretching from wall to wall across a room. The line runs from left to right. The left-hand wall represents verbal abuse. Verbal abuse includes name calling, screaming and yelling, threats, and sarcasm. Threatening postures and gestures (making a fist, acting as though you are going to hit somebody, pointing a weapon) combined with verbal abuse are somewhere in the middle of the line. The right-hand wall represents physical violence (punching, slapping, shoving) which may result in injury or death. It is all violence.

. . . .

SELF-TEST

1. Look at the list below. Put a check mark (✔) beside the type of violence you have used.

    ❑ Name calling   ❑ Screaming and yelling

    ❑ Sarcasm   ❑ Threatening postures

    ❑ Threats   ❑ Threatening gestures

    ❑ Punching, slapping, shoving

2. Have you ever been the target of physical or verbal violence?

    YES   NO

3. If you answered "yes" to question #2, explain in a few words how being a target of physical or verbal violence made you feel.

4. Think of the last time you were angry. Did you use verbal violence (angry words, screaming, and yelling)? Did you make violent threats or use threatening postures? Did you use physical violence? Look at the violence diagram below. Put a check mark (✔) at the place on the line that best describes the kind of violence you used on that occasion.

V	I	O	L	E	N	C	E

← Verbal Threats   Violent Threats/Postures   Physical Violence →

. . . .

Innocent Victims of Teen Anger

Some teens who, themselves, do not have a problem with anger end up as innocent victims of teens whose anger is out of control. The killings in 1999 at Columbine High School in Colorado is an example. Other innocent victims include teens in large cities all over the country who become targets for, and innocent victims of, teen gangs whose members are addicted to anger and rage. Often, the victims then develop a problem with anger as a result of having been victimized. It is almost as though the gangs carry anger and rage like a virus among them, then through their violence infect others with the same destructive behavior. In some instances, organized gangs of angry teens have destroyed the trust of entire communities. And generation after generation, the violence goes on.

· ·

SELF-TEST

1. Can you trace your anger problem back to a time that you were a victim of some other teen's angry behavior?

    YES   NO

2. Were you ever a victim of gang violence?

    YES   NO

3. If you answered "yes" to either question #1 or question #2, write down in a few words how that made you feel.

· ·

Resentment and Hate

Resentment and hate are forms of anger. Resentment is a milder form. Hate is the most intense form of anger. People who hate show intense anger toward people and things they hate. Sometimes they hate whole groups of people. That is called race hate or ethnic hate. Some people hate those who have a different sexual preference. Some people hate those who practice a different religious belief.

Most people who hate have an anger habit, or are even addicted to anger. They are anger addicts who use racial or ethnic groups or those with a different sexual preference or religious belief as targets for their anger.

. . . .

SELF-TEST

1. Have you used racial or ethnic groups as targets for your anger? Have you used people with a different sexual preference, or with a different religious belief as targets for your anger?

YES   NO

. . . .

How Anger is Like a Drug

Addiction to drugs such as alcohol or meth (methadrine or methamphetamine) is known by certain signs and symptoms. Anger is like a drug. You can develop an anger habit the way some people develop a drug habit. You can even become addicted to anger. For someone who uses anger like a drug, getting angry is like using cocaine or meth, then using heroin right after. The angry outburst is like a cocaine or meth rush. Cocaine and meth cause the brain to produce a certain chemical. The chemical causes the adrenal glands to send a lot of adrenaline into the bloodstream. It fills you with energy and makes you feel powerful. When the anger subsides, the adrenaline stops. Then the brain produces a different chemical called endorphin. The endorphin chemical is a lot like heroin. So you end up feeling relaxed and calm, the way heroin makes people feel. The anger makes you feel a kind of "high" feeling which is very much like the "high" produced by drugs.

MESSAGE FROM JACK

Hi. My name is Jack. I'm sixteen. My drug of choice was anger, but I also used and abused alcohol. I used other drugs too. Meth, mostly. I know some of you can relate. I've been clean and sober a while now. I know some of you understand what I'm saying, because you've had problems with alcohol and drugs too. But if you've never had an alcohol or drug hangover, then you won't understand how anger is like a drug, the way I can understand it. It's easy for me. I've had a lot of hangovers from alcohol and drugs. I had one hangover that lasted all day! I've had anger hangovers that lasted all day too. They felt just like alcohol hangovers. They made me feel totally tired out. I'd wake up in the morning feeling guilty, and stupid too. To me, anger hangovers were worse than alcohol and drug hangovers. With alcohol and drug hangovers, I didn't always remember what I did and said. That way, I could blame my behavior on the alcohol or the meth. I've heard a lot of other people say the same thing at Pathways to Peace meetings.

Jack

How People Get Addicted to Anger

Here's how you develop an anger habit or anger addiction: You use anger over and over, and experience a "high" each time you use it. The brain enjoys the high and wants to repeat it. You continue getting high on anger over and over again. Finally you develop an anger habit, because you get addicted to the "high" feeling produced by the anger.

Other Ways Anger is Like a Drug

Drug addicts develop a high tolerance to their drug. They need more and more of the drug to feel the same effect. High tolerance to any drug is one of the signs or symptoms of addiction to the drug.

Alcoholics are addicted to the drug called alcohol. They develop a high tolerance for alcohol. They also suffer a rebound effect from the drug. The rebound effect is another sign of addiction to a drug. People who have the rebound effect feel hungover the next day. They feel shaky and tired. They feel guilt, shame, and free-floating fear. Free-floating fear means you're in a state of fear much of the time, the kind of fear which is hard to identify and name. Guilt, shame, and free-floating fear are signs of addiction to a drug.

Angry people get drunk on anger. Like alcoholics, angry people develop a high tolerance to their drug: anger. They need to use more and more anger to feel high. Like alcoholics, they suffer a rebound effect. Anger addicts have anger and rage hangovers. They feel shaky and tired the morning after. They feel guilt, shame, and free-floating fear. Meth addicts and cocaine users feel those same bad feelings the morning after using a lot of meth or cocaine.

. . . .

SELF-TEST

1. You can develop an anger habit the way some people develop a drug habit.

    TRUE   FALSE

2. Getting angry is like using meth or cocaine, then using heroin right after.

    TRUE   FALSE

3. According to the text, high tolerance is a sign, or symptom, of addiction to drugs, and is also a sign of addiction to anger. In a few words, explain what is meant by "high tolerance."

4. People who use drugs such as alcohol or meth often experience a rebound effect. In a few words, explain the "rebound effect."

. . . .

Excessive Anger as Learned Behavior

You didn't have to learn how to be angry, but you had to learn to abuse anger. You were born with the ability to use anger. You used that ability when you were a baby. If you were hungry, you felt discomfort. If you weren't fed, you got frustrated. Hunger and frustration triggered your anger. You yelled and cried, kicked and screamed. Then someone fed you. Or you went to sleep. If you went to sleep hungry, you probably woke up angry again. Later you learned other ways to get your needs met. You learned other ways to deal with hunger, and you learned other ways to deal with frustration and other anger triggers. But you didn't forget how to use anger.

How Did You Learn Your Anger Habit?

You learned your anger habit from other people. You may have learned it from one or both of your parents, or from your brothers or sisters. You probably learned some of the pattern from kids you grew up with. You learned it from what you saw and heard others do. You learned some of your anger from television and movies, and from books and video games.

You learned a major part of your anger pattern from the results you got when you used anger. You felt pleasure when you got angry. You felt powerful. You copped a high. It felt almost as though you had used a powerful drug. Each time you felt an anger high, your brain recorded a memory of

MESSAGE FROM SEAN

One more thing. Finding out how you learned your anger habit and who you learned your anger habit from, isn't about blaming. It's about understanding the problem. The person or persons you learned it from, it's not their problem. It's yours. Bill wanted me to jump in and make that clear.

Sean

the experience in the pleasure center of your brain. An automatic behavior track began to develop in your brain, like a track on a CD. You could say an anger track began to develop. The anger track grew stronger each time you felt an anger high. Eventually anger became a permanent behavior track laid down in your brain, like a certain track on a music CD. Once the anger track was laid down, it didn't take much to make it play, did it? Something happened in your surroundings, or someone said something or did something that made you feel powerless, and you got angry. Just like pressing the Start button on a CD player, right?

You probably didn't have negative results in the beginning. Otherwise you probably wouldn't have developed an anger habit in the first place. You used angry behavior to feel powerful, and it worked. You didn't lose anything. You didn't get in trouble at home or in school. You didn't get arrested and lose your freedom. You didn't get hurt. You used anger and received only pleasure, seldom pain. You were consistently rewarded with pleasure. That's how you learned much of your anger habit.

> *You know you have an anger habit or are addicted to anger when*
> *you start using anger to try to solve all your problems.*

. . . .

SELF-TEST

1. Look at the list of sentences below. Circle the sentences that are true.

   Excessive anger is a learned behavior.

   You were born with an anger habit.

   You learned your anger from other people.

   You learned some of your anger from kids you grew up with.

2. Look at the list below. Circle the people or things on the list from whom or from which you think you learned your anger pattern.

My mother	My sister
My father	My brother
Kids I hung out with	Violent movies, video games, or books

. . . .

How People From Non-Violent Homes Develop

a Serious Problem With Anger

Not every teen who has a serious anger problem grew up in violent surroundings. For some, their parents were together, not divorced. They had non-violent friends. They didn't abuse alcohol or other drugs. They didn't watch violent movies or play violent games. In fact, some teens with a serious anger problem or anger addiction seem to have grown up in ideal surroundings. So why did they develop a serious anger problem? Read the message from Lisa and find out.

Styles of Anger

Outward Focus

Some people express anger openly. They are loud and aggressive. The results they suffer are also easily seen. They hurt others, then end up in a detention center or in jail. They get beat up. Sometimes they hurt themselves.

Inward Focus

Other people use a different style. They express their anger inwardly. They aren't as likely to say or do angry things. They aren't as likely to damage property. Their negative results are not as easily seen. Often, people who use the inward focus suffer from severe depression. Sometimes they do physical harm to themselves. Sometimes they even commit suicide. In later life, they often develop ulcers and high blood pressure.

. . . .

MESSAGE FROM LISA

Hi, my name is Lisa. I have an anger habit. I'm from Tulsa. I'm sixteen. I had two loving parents who stayed together. They argued sometimes, but never fought. My parents never abused me. I never saw violence in my home. I never suffered trauma, like some of my friends have. I didn't have violent friends. I didn't watch a lot of violent movies and didn't play violent video games. I was never a victim of violence; yet I developed a problem with anger. How come? A recovering anger addict called Barbara is my mentor. She explained it to me this way. She said there are two types of people with anger problems. One type is kind of set up for anger problems, because of things that happened to them or because of things they saw. Barbara said people who grow up in violent surroundings fit into this group. They feel powerless and use anger to feel powerful. They develop a problem with anger fast. The second type is different. Barbara told me they don't come from violent homes. They never had trauma in their lives. They don't start out feeling as powerless as the first type. They don't have as much fear and tension. They don't develop a problem with anger as fast as the first group. But this type does find out that anger makes them feel high. They repeat the behavior over and over; finally, they get hooked on the high. They get addicted to the adrenaline rush. Barbara says I fit into that group.

Lisa

1. Circle the style of anger listed below that best describes your anger style.

   Outward focus

   Inward focus

2. List some of the consequences you have suffered because of your angry behavior.

· ·

The Masks Anger Wears

Anger Disguised as Sarcasm

Sarcasm is a mask. Don't be fooled. Sarcasm often is anger. It causes harm. It hurts people's feelings. Using sarcasm often leads to violent behavior.

· ·

SELF-TEST

1. Do you use sarcasm?

   YES   NO

2. Have you ever been the target of sarcasm?

   YES   NO

3. If you have ever been the target of someone's sarcasm, explain in a few words how it made you feel.

· ·

Anger is often disguised as humor. Making jokes that hurt other people's feelings is an example of anger disguised as humor.

. . . .

SELF-TEST

1. Do you disguise your anger with humor? Do you do "funny" things that in some way hurt others? Do you say "funny" things that cause others emotional pain?

YES   NO

. . . .

Anger Disguised as "Teasing" and "Button Pushing"

Some angry people use teasing or button pushing to hurt others. You are using button pushing when you deliberately say or do things that you know will cause a strong reaction.

. . . .

SELF-TEST

1. Do you tease people and deliberately push people's buttons?

YES   NO

. . . .

Anger and Grief

> **MESSAGE FROM BRENDA**
>
> *I'm Brenda. I'm sixteen and I have a problem with anger. I didn't know how much power words have. I didn't know how much damage words could do. I didn't know how much pain my screaming and yelling caused other people. I didn't know how much damage my sarcasm caused. Later when I started getting a handle on my anger problem, I remembered that people said things to me when I was a little kid that really hurt. My family said things. My mother sometimes called me stupid. "You're stupid, Brenda!" she'd scream. Every time she said it, it felt like a knife in my heart. Then my brother and sister would get in on it too. "Yeah. You're stupid, Brenda!" they'd yell. Other kids said things too that hurt me. That type of anger became a part of my anger problem. I got real good at using words like knives to cut people with. Finally I became aware of what I was doing. I'm still struggling with my anger, but now I don't use words to hurt people anymore. Oh, once in a while it still happens. I go to Pathways to Peace meetings, and Pathways to Peace is about being honest. So I have to try to be honest with you. But now when the words come out like knives, I try to apologize right away.*
>
> *Brenda*

Grief means "deep sorrow." When you grieve, you suffer strong feelings of loss. If someone you love died, you would suffer grief. The death of a loved one is a great loss. The death of a parent, or the death of a close friend, would cause you grief. If someone you love leaves you, you would suffer grief. The death of a favorite pet would also cause you grief. Any time you lose something you greatly value, you will suffer grief. When alcoholics and drug addicts stop using alcohol and drugs, they also suffer grief. They grieve the loss of their drug(s) of choice.

Grief is a process. All people go through the same process when they grieve the loss of someone or something they love or greatly value. You may have lost a parent or a friend because they died. You may have lost a parent because of abandonment or divorce. You may have lost your self-respect or your freedom because of something you did. Losses such as these would undoubtedly cause you grief.

The Five Stages of the Grief Process

There are five stages in the grief process:

1. Denial
2. Anger
3. Bargaining
4. Depression
5. Acceptance

For our purposes, we focus on the first two stages of this process.

The Denial Stage of the Grief Process

The first stage in the grief process is called **Denial**. When you lose something you greatly value, at first you can't believe it happened. You want to deny the loss. The denial stage of the grief process usually passes quickly. The bargaining stage usually passes fairly quickly too. The depression stage may last a long time. It can take one to three years to reach the acceptance stage of the grief process. But sometimes people get stuck in the process. Although it is important to understand the entire grief process, as a person with an anger problem it is especially important to understand the anger stage of the process.

The Anger Stage of the Grief Process

Anger is the second stage of the grief process. In this stage, you see that the loss is real. You see that it really happened, and that makes you angry. You may even rage at the loss.

You may have suffered a great loss some time in the past. Notice that one of the stages of the grief process is **Depression**. Depression is an anger trigger because depression makes you feel powerless. You may be stuck in the anger stage of the grief process. You may have been using anger for a very long time, to fight depression due to grief. It may be the reason you developed an anger habit to begin with.

· ·

SELF-TEST

1. Have you experienced the loss of one or both of your parents through death, or abandonment, or divorce?

   YES   NO

2. Have you experienced the loss of a favorite pet?

   YES   NO

· ·

MESSAGE FROM AL

Hi. My name is Al, and I have a problem with anger. I'm fifteen years old. When I was seven, my mother died in a car accident. I went through the denial stage in just a few days. Then the anger started, and I got stuck there. Oh, I did some bargaining too. I tried to make a bargain with God. I said I'd never do anything bad ever again if only my mom would come back. Then the depression started. I didn't know what to do about that, so I jumped back into anger. That worked. It got me out of depression. Every time I started to feel depressed, I'd get angry instead. My anger caused me problems in school and with my family and friends. But I didn't care. At least I wasn't depressed anymore. I had bad consequences because of my angry behavior, but the trade-off seemed like a good deal. When I was sixteen, they put me in the alternative education program, and I had to go to school at night. That sucked. Then I started going to the school counselor. She helped me understand what was going on. I started going to a Pathways to Peace group too, near my house, where some other teens like me went for help with their problem. I changed my behavior for the better, and things in my life got a lot better too. I'm still going to my counselor and to my meetings.

Al

CHAPTER FIVE

Trauma and the Roots of Anger and Rage

Trauma Involving Violent Events

Some people who develop an anger problem were abused as children. Some were beaten. Some were sexually abused. Some suffered trauma as a result of having witnessed violent events. The word "trauma" means severe injury. People who have suffered severe injury to their body have experienced physical trauma. People who have seen something that caused severe physical injury to another person have experienced severe emotional injury. Of course, a person who suffers severe injury to the body may also have experienced severe injury to the emotions. When people suffer emotional trauma, they often end up with what is called Post Traumatic Stress Disorder, or PTSD. PTSD is known by certain symptoms or signs. Some of the common symptoms or signs of PTSD include:

- Insomnia (trouble sleeping)
- Nightmares and night sweats
- High levels of anxiety and fear
- Extremely high levels of internal tension
- Depression
- Anger

Notice that one of the common symptoms of PTSD is anger. The anger associated with PTSD is usually a very intense form of anger, often leading to violence. The anger associated with PTSD often lasts a very long time. At first the anger may be aimed only at the person or persons responsible for the trauma. Later, PTSD victims develop a pattern of anger that becomes generalized. They become angry at people and things that have nothing to do with the event that caused them to suffer symptoms of PTSD.

Self-Blame and PTSD

Sometimes people suffering from PTSD end up blaming themselves for the traumatic event they witnessed or experienced. They come to believe, wrongly, that they could have done something to keep the awful event from happening. They are not to blame.

Many angry people were abandoned when they were children by one or both parents. Abandonment is another form of trauma. People who have been abandoned feel rejected and afraid. Abandonment makes it hard to predict what is going to happen. Often children who are abandoned blame themselves for what happened. They come to believe that, somehow, it was their fault. They may think that there is something wrong with them. But once again, they are not at fault and are not to blame. They feel defective. Later these feelings became triggers for anger and rage.

Lasting Effects of Trauma

The trauma suffered by some people during childhood can have lifelong effects. The environment they lived in may have been like a war zone. There was constant tension in their lives. The constant tension raised their inner tension above the normal level. This higher level of inner tension became permanent. People who grow up in violent surroundings often suffer from PTSD.

(Continued on next page)

from shock. Then I started coming out of it.

I went to live with my aunt. She helped me get over the worst of the shock. But I should have been seen by a counselor too. After a while, I started to think that the whole thing was my fault. I was so angry with myself! I though maybe I could've done something to keep it from happening. "Vince!," I'd yell at myself, "why didn't you reach over the seat and take the gun away from her?"

Until I started going to a counselor—it was a long time after it happened—I didn't realize how much my anger was connected to what I saw that night in the grocery store parking lot. I still see pictures in my mind of what happened. Usually, it's at night after dark. Sometimes I even think I hear the sound of the gun going off. I start to sweat and my stomach gets real tight. My counselor says those are flashbacks. She says a lot of people with PTSD have flashbacks. Sometimes I have nightmares. I wake up sweating and scared, and thinking it's—that night. It happened ten years ago, but I still think about it. Not on purpose. It just pops into my mind. My counselor says people who suffer from trauma often have nightmares. She says it's another sign of PTSD. I've been going to my counselor for three years. I'm not over the PTSD yet, but I feel a lot better than I did. My nightmares aren't as scary. I sleep better now. And my anger is not anywhere near as bad as it used to be. The best part is that I don't try to justify my anger anymore by blaming it on my PTSD. Pathways to Peace has taught me that anger and rage are never justified, no matter how righteous the cause.

Vince

If the symptoms of PTSD go untreated, the anger and other symptoms of PTSD may last a lifetime.

High Levels of Inner Tension and Anger

Everything we know about the kind of ongoing, intense anger that causes harm to others and that leads to consequences for angry people shows a connection to a very high level of inner tension. We have seen that trauma is often the cause of the high level of inner tension some angry people experience. The inner tension level of people who have problems with anger and rage is higher than normal. The higher-than-normal tension level contributes to the development of anger problems. The increased tension level also accounts for the high number of angry people who also have problems with alcohol and other drugs, and who use alcohol and other drugs to try to lower their tension level. People with anger problems learn to use anger to relieve their tension.

You may be one of those who suffered trauma during childhood. Your home may have been like a war zone. If so, you can point at these things as part of the cause of your excessive use of anger. Yet, it would be self-defeating to use an abusive childhood as an excuse for using violence and rage in the present. No matter what was done to us in the past, we are responsible for what we do in the present. We are responsible for the harm we have done to ourselves. We must come to believe that there is no excuse for violence.

What Vince saw was one of the worst things anyone could ever see. That it involved the violent death of his father and that his mother was the one responsible made it all the worse for Vince. It is no wonder that Vince ended up with Post Traumatic Stress

Disorder. When people witness or experience violent events and are physically very close to what happened, they will suffer the type of severe trauma Vince suffered and will end up with Post Traumatic Stress Disorder, or PTSD. If you have experienced anything like what Vince went through, and aren't seeing a professional counselor, you need to find a counselor now. Make sure you find a counselor who is trained in helping people who suffer from PTSD. With professional help, you can learn to deal effectively with the symptoms of PTSD. Then you will be able to deal more effectively with your anger problem.

. . . .

SELF-TEST

1. Have you ever had something happen to you, or ever seen something happen to someone else, that made you feel the way Vince felt?

   YES   NO

2. Have you ever suffered from any of the symptoms of PTSD?

   YES   NO

3. If you have suffered emotional trauma, you should get help from a professional counselor.

   TRUE   FALSE

4. The tension level of people who have a problem with anger is higher than normal.

   TRUE   FALSE

5. Left untreated, the anger associated with PTSD may last a lifetime.

   TRUE   FALSE

. . . .

Sexual Abuse as Trauma

Sexual abuse is a form of trauma. Some teens who have been sexually abused also suffer from PTSD. You might have been sexually molested as a child or have been molested more recently, after you entered your teens. Even if you have never been sexually molested, you should read this part of *Managing Teen Anger and Violence*.

Chances are, you know someone who has been molested. With what you learn in this part of the workbook, you could help that person get the help they need.

If you were ever sexually abused, whether as a child or since you entered your teens, it is extremely likely that you would benefit from professional counseling. If you have experienced any of the forms of sexual abuse described below, and are not now receiving professional help about sexual abuse issues, it is strongly suggested that you become involved in professional counseling as soon as possible. Please do it now. Don't wait. Left untreated, issues of sexual abuse could keep you stuck in anger and rage indefinitely. With help, you can overcome these issues and learn how to effectively manage your anger.

Types of Sexual Abuse

Rape

There are many types of sexual abuse. Rape is one type. Often the rape victim is subjected to physical violence resulting in severe physical injury. Even if the victim is not subjected to physical injury, he or she will suffer extreme emotional harm.

A child, teenager, or adult who has been forced to have sexual relations with someone, no matter what the attacker's age or gender, is a victim of rape. The attacker is a rapist. Rape is a crime punishable by imprisonment. Rape is an act of violence. It is violence in its very worst form. People who have been raped have suffered one of the worst forms of trauma. Undoubtedly, any child or teen who has been raped will end up with severe PTSD issues.

The laws differ somewhat, but most states define a child as someone under the age of eighteen, an adult as someone eighteen years old or older. A person under the age of eighteen who has been forced to have sexual relations is a victim of rape. Even if a person under the age of eighteen (whether male or female) agrees to have sexual relations with someone older than themselves, in the eyes of the law he or she is a victim of rape. This is true in most states in the U.S., if one of the sex partners is eighteen or over. In some states, it may be age sixteen or over. In either case, the older sex partner is considered a rapist. This type of rape, where sex relations have been consensual (which means both parties agree to have sex with each other), is sometimes called "statutory rape."

Rapists come from all social, ethnic, and economic backgrounds. "Perpetrator" is the term often used to describe the rapist. The perpetrator, or rapist, may be a complete stranger. But the perpetrator is sometimes a friend of the victim, or a friend of the victim's family. The perpetrator may even be a close family member, the victim's brother, sister, or grandparent. The perpetrator may even be the victim's father or mother. When the perpetrator is a close relative, the offense is referred to as "incest rape."

Date Rape

This category of rape is recognized as a criminal offense and usually involves a male offender. Date rape may involve threats of violence to force the victim into agreeing to have sexual relations. Sometimes the perpetrator of date rape drugs the victim, so that the victim will be unable to resist sexual advances. Alcohol is the drug most widely used by perpetrators of date rape. Sometimes the perpetrator uses alcohol combined with another type of drug in order to break down his victim's defenses. Sometimes, both the victim and the perpetrator are under the influence of alcohol or other drugs. When a teen or adult says "no" to sexual relations and the other person uses any of the tactics mentioned above to force the victim to have sexual relations, date rape is the result. Anyone who has been the victim of date rape should report the offense to the appropriate authorities.

As was pointed out earlier, rape is a form of trauma. If the incidence of rape is of the type that involves violence or threats of violence, the victim will certainly end up traumatized by the event. Even when physical violence is not present, the victim will very likely suffer serious trauma as a result. The rape victim will experience symptoms of Post Traumatic Stress Disorder, or PTSD. The symptoms of PTSD caused by rape are the same as those caused by being a victim of other kinds of violence, or by seeing someone else victimized by violence: insomnia, nightmares, night sweats, high levels of anxiety and fear, and extremely high levels of internal tension, depression, and anger.

· ·

SELF-TEST

1. Sexual abuse is a form of trauma.

    TRUE   FALSE

2. Someone who has been raped will probably not develop Post Traumatic Stress Disorder.

    TRUE   FALSE

3. Rape always involves physical violence to the victim.

    TRUE   FALSE

· ·

Sexual Molestation

Sexual molestation is another form of sexual abuse. The perpetrator of the type of sexual abuse called sexual molestation may be either male or female. The perpetrator may be a teenager or an adult. In rare cases the perpetrator may be a child under the age of thirteen. Perpetrators of sexual molestation may come from any walk of life, from any income level or ethnic group. Most perpetrators of sexual molestation are adult males, but some are women. Some perpetrators of sexual molestation are teenagers. The victim of sexual molestation may be an adult, a teen, or a child.

Types of Sexual Molestation

Sexual molestation takes many forms. Generally, it involves any physical contact on the part of the perpetrator with a victim's sexual parts. Touching, kissing, petting, or hugging in a way the victim, or a court of law, would deem sexual in nature are all forms of sexual molestation.

Pedophilia

The desire to have sexual relations with children is a mental disorder called Pedophilia. Those who suffer from this disorder are called pedophiles. While some pedophiles are women, most are men. Some pedophiles are teenagers and may be either male or female. Not all pedophiles actually follow through with their desire to have sexual relations with children. When a pedophile acts on his or her desire to have sexual relations with children, they are called child molesters.

Most pedophiles who become child molesters are known to their victims. Often the perpetrator is a family friend, or even a relative such as an uncle or an aunt, a grandparent, or an older cousin. Sometimes a child is molested by his or her father or mother, or by a sister or brother. When a child is molested by a close relative, it is called incest. In the U.S. incest is a criminal offense even when the parties involved are adults and both agree without coercion to have sexual relations.

Child molesters come from all social classes and ethnic backgrounds. As stated earlier, they may be either men or women, though most are men. Some child molesters are heterosexual, meaning they prefer to have sexual relations with children of the opposite sex. Male child molesters who are heterosexual would prefer to have sexual relations with girls; female child molesters who are heterosexual would prefer boys. Male child molesters who are homosexual by orientation would prefer to have sex with male children; female molesters who are lesbians prefer female children.

Victims of Child Molestation

Victims of child molestation also come from all backgrounds. Victims' ages also vary. Some victims of child molestation are under a year old, some are from one to twelve years of age. Some victims of molestation may be in their early to mid-teens. The effect of being sexually abused has a lasting and extremely negative effect, no matter what the victim's age. But the effect can be especially devastating for a teenager. The effect on the psychological development of teens who have been molested is always negative. The damaging effects of sexual molestation on self-image and feelings of self-worth can last throughout a teen's lifetime.

Even adult men and women can be victims of molestation. Perpetrators who stop short of raping their victims are still guilty of sexual abuse, and may be categorized as sexual molesters. The emotional injury suffered by their victims is considerable and could result in the development of Post Traumatic Stress Disorder.

How Pedophiles Operate

Although pedophiles are seen as persons who are mentally ill, that does not mean that they are not responsible when they cross over the line and become molesters. They most certainly are responsible. There is absolutely no excuse for their actions.

Pedophiles who become child molesters often seek and find work in or near environments where they are likely to encounter children. They may seek work in a factory or office, for example, which is near a school playground. Sometimes a child molester may own a business that caters to children—for example, a small neighborhood store where candy is sold. Or the molester may work in the toy department of a large store. Some child molesters, both male and female, seek volunteer work in organizations that cater especially to children or teens, such as Boy Scouts or Girl Scouts. Some try to find work in youth centers.

As mentioned earlier, a child molester may be a friend of his victim, or a friend of an intended victim's family. In such cases, the child molester may do things for the family or for the intended victim in order to gain their trust. The molester might volunteer to "babysit" for the parents, if the intended victim is very young, say under thirteen years old. Child molesters have also been known to hang around video arcades. They occasionally offer money to children and teens who need it to continue to use the machines.

Many child molesters prefer victims who are in their teens and, therefore, more sexually mature. They often set up their teen victims by offering them alcohol or other drugs. They may invite teen victims to "private parties" at their house. Sometimes child molesters work together. For example, a man and woman might work together as a team to lure children and teens into their house in order to sexually molest them. Sometimes homosexuals work together, sometimes lesbians do. Some molesters use pornography as a way to entice teenage victims. Often, alcohol and drugs are used along with pornography to set teens up. A ploy often used by molesters who own businesses is to offer the victim a job. Usually, the job is too easy and the pay too high. Sometimes the child molester will "loan" money to a teen victim. These schemes, and other schemes as well, are used to set the victim up. First, the molester gains the trust of the intended victim. Then the molester makes the intended victim feel obligated in some way. Then the nice man or woman who seemed to care so much, and seemed so generous and kind, attacks. Child molestation does not often involve violence or threats of violence. Enticement is the child molester's primary weapon.

MESSAGE FROM SEAN

In my story in Chapter One, I talked about when I was molested. I didn't say much. As I said, I don't like to talk about it. Just thinking about it makes me want to throw up. The pedophile who molested me didn't look weird. That's the first thing you gotta learn. They look like any other guy, usually. He was a Vietnam vet, even showed me his medals. He owned a little grocery store in my neighborhood. Sometimes I stopped there for ice cream. I'll call him John. One time I stopped to buy an ice cream cone, and when I put my money on the counter, he said, "Nah, this one's on me." Couldn't pass that up, right? Free ice cream. I thanked him and went out the door happy. After a few more free ice cream cones, he told me I could earn some more free ice cream cones, even some money, if I'd help him out a little around the store. You know, take out the garbage, sweep the floor. Easy stuff, simple stuff. Well, pretty soon I was working for John every day, for about an hour after school. Then one day he said, "Hey, Sean, how 'bout helping me put some canned goods on the shelves in the back room? It won't take long, and you can earn a couple extra dollars." I said, sure, why not? Then John went and closed and locked the door, and hung the "Closed" sign in the window. I thought that was a little strange, because it was about half an hour before he usually closed up. I followed John to the back room, and he closed that door too. That's when it happened. I'm not going to tell you the details—I can't, it makes me too angry! The creep molested me, leave it at that. Finally, a long time after, as I said in my story, I went and got counseling. I didn't tell my mom right away, I didn't tell anybody. I felt so embarrassed, and for some stupid reason so ashamed.

I'm not over it yet. I still have nightmares and, at times, I still blame myself. I'm still angry at myself for being so stupid. I didn't understand how he'd been setting me up for it with those free ice cream cones. But I was only ten years old! What did I know? If anything like that ever happened to you, don't blame yourself. The one who molested you is the one to blame. After a while, I told my mom what happened. Lucky for me, she believed me. Some parents don't, especially if the guilty party happens to be a friend or relative. She didn't confront John herself. She went to the cops. Nothing was done about it right away. It's really hard to get a conviction because there's usually no witnesses and it ends up being a kid's word against the adult offender's. But about a year later the guy was caught in the act by the father of another kid. There were three other victims, all boys about ten years old, who stepped forward too. This time, there was a conviction. The guy went to prison for a couple of years. He did it again when he got out, and now he's in prison again. That's the way they are. Most of them never change.

Here's something that'll make you want to go get help from a counselor, if you haven't already. Do you know what sometimes happens to kids and teens who've been sexually

---

abused and don't get help? They sometimes end up becoming sexual abusers themselves. Okay, that's it. Don't ask me to talk about this crap again!

Sean

. . . .

SELF-TEST

1. Sexual molestation is a type of sexual abuse.

   TRUE   FALSE

2. Child molesters are always adult men.

   TRUE   FALSE

3. Child molesters come from all walks of life and all ethnic groups.

   TRUE   FALSE

4. All pedophiles are child molesters.

   TRUE   FALSE

5. According to Sean in the message above, people who have been molested should seek professional help. Those who don't get help sometimes become child molesters themselves.

   TRUE   FALSE

6. Victims of sexual molestation may develop Post Traumatic Stress Disorder.

   TRUE   FALSE

7. The child molester's primary weapon is:

   VIOLENCE   ENTICEMENT

. . . .

PART TWO

Understanding the Recovery Process

CHAPTER SIX

The Eight Parts of the Whole Self

Your whole self is made up of eight vital parts. The eight vital parts are interactive and interdependent. Each part depends on the other seven parts, and each part acts on each of the other parts. How each of these vital parts functions will determine how well the whole self works. You need to change and grow in each of your eight parts, in order to be happy in your recovery from your anger habit. The eight parts of your whole self are:

1. **Biological** (your body)
2. **Environmental** (your surroundings)
3. **Behavioral** (your actions, everything you do)
4. **Skills** (what you are good at, what you have learned)
5. **Values/Goals** (what is important to you, what you want to be or do)
6. **Beliefs** (your attitudes about yourself and your world, what you believe is true)
7. **Mission/Identity** (your purpose in life, why you are here)
8. **Spiritual** (the part of you that makes you feel connected to others, to the universe, and to the Higher Power of your understanding)

The Eight Parts Compared to an Eight-Cylinder Car

One way to understand the eight parts of the whole self is by comparing the whole self to an eight-cylinder car. To function fully and well, all eight cylinders must be in good shape. Each cylinder must cooperate and do its job. If all the cylinders cooperate, the car will take you where you want to go.

But what if one cylinder develops a problem? What if it becomes damaged? That cylinder will function poorly. The damaged cylinder will be unable to cooperate well with the rest of the cylinders. It will throw everything out of balance and cause the whole car to miss and lurch, and lose power. Left unattended, the condition of the damaged cylinder will get worse and worse. The damaged cylinder will have a negative effect on the rest of the cylinders. It will cause the other cylinders to work too hard. Soon another cylinder will develop problems, then another, and another. Finally the whole car will break down. The same is true of the recovery process. Full recovery means recovery of the whole self. It means recovery of all eight parts.

Parable of the Flower

Another way to understand the eight vital parts is by comparing the whole self to an eight-petal flower. To be whole and healthy, all eight petals must be healthy. Each petal must cooperate and do its job. If all the petals cooperate, the flower will thrive and grow.

But what if one petal becomes diseased? The diseased petal will function poorly. It will be unable to cooperate, unable to stay fully open along with the rest of the petals. If untreated, the diseased petal will close up. This will affect the rest of the petals. Soon they will close up too. Then the entire flower will close up like an angry fist. Then all light will be shut out; the flower will wilt. Closing up tighter and tighter, the flower will die.

> **MESSAGE FROM RAYMOND**
>
> *I'm Raymond. I'm sixteen. I'm a Skin. That's short for Redskin. I can call myself that, because I'm a Native American. But don't you call me by that name—Skin. Unless you're one yourself. Yep, I've got ethnic rage too. But not like before, not even close. I buried that hatchet.*
>
> *I never used to exercise. Just sat around the trailer and watched TV and drank beer. I didn't eat right. I was sick with colds all winter. I didn't sleep well and felt tired all the time. I was way out of shape. I looked like some old Indian guy about forty—the ones my friends and I call "big bellies." I had a gut and my arms and legs were flabby. Every time I looked in the mirror, my feelings about myself sank lower because I didn't like what I saw. My counselor calls it low self-esteem. It was one of my major anger triggers. Then I started working out with one of the guys in my Pathways to Peace meeting. He made a gym in his garage. I started exercising, eating right, and sleeping better. I lost weight and looked better. As soon as I got in shape, I felt better about myself. My self-esteem got better. Now I feel good about how I look.*
>
> *Raymond*

Part One – Biological

Your health is determined in large part by what you eat and by what you do with your body. Nutrition is an extremely important part of the process of recovery from an anger habit. A well-balanced diet of nutritious food will help to create a healthy body. A poorly balanced diet of junk food will create a unhealthy body. Overeating will cause you to gain weight, which may cause you to feel low self-esteem. Feelings of low self-esteem can be a major anger trigger. All of the other vital parts influence the condition of the body.

Your body also needs rest and sleep. Most people need from six to nine hours sleep each night, in order to feel rested and alert. Because you are growing so fast, you often need as much as 10 hours sleep. Just a day or two without adequate sleep will have a negative effect on how you feel and how you function. It will cause your tension level to rise. That will increase your sensitivity to frustration and anxiety, which are anger triggers.

Obviously, your body is important. If you are in good physical health, you feel good. When you feel good, you are more likely to use good behavior.

. . . .

SELF-TEST

1. According to the text, the whole self has eight parts and is like an eight-cylinder car engine.

TRUE   FALSE

2. Are you "way out of shape," as Raymond said he once was?

YES   NO

3. If you answered "yes" to question #2, explain in a few words what you could do to get in shape.

. . . .

Part Two – Environmental

Your Outer Environment

You live in relationship to people, places, and things. The sum total of these people, places, and things is your outer environment. In fact you could not live alone and stay alive. You could not survive without having certain people, places, and things in your life.

The people, places, and things you choose in your outer environment affect the health of your body. They affect how you behave. They affect what skills you will develop. They affect your values and goals, your beliefs, and your sense of mission. They affect your spirituality. People, places, and things affect you in a positive way, or they affect you in a negative way.

Your Inner Environment

Your mind is another kind of environment. Your mind contains your thoughts. Your mind also contains your spirituality, your sense of mission, your beliefs, your values, your goals, your skills, and all of your automatic behaviors. The sum total of all these things is your inner environment. Your inner environment affects your outer environment. Your outer environment, in turn, affects your inner environment.

. . . .

SELF-TEST

1. Name the two ways people, places, and things influence you.

2. List three people, places, and things in your life that could have a bad influence on your recovery from your anger problem.

> **MESSAGE FROM JEFF**
>
> *I'm Jeff, and I have a big problem with anger. I'm from Detroit. All of my friends were like me–angry all the time. They came from angry homes. Alcoholic homes. Abusive homes. When I started my recovery from my anger problem, I was in denial about how these things affected me. It took me a long time and a bunch of relapses to finally admit I had to change some of the things in my outer and my inner environment. Finally, I saw the bad influence my old friends had on me. I saw the bad influence they had on my mind, on my thoughts, on my beliefs, and on my attitudes and values and on my behaviors. Then I saw the bad influence certain places and things had on me. I stopped hanging out with my old friends. I stopped hanging out in the old places. And I stopped holding on to the old things.*
>
> *It was hard to make the changes, especially changing my friends and making new ones. But I had to, in order to change my actions and stay out of trouble. After I started going to my Pathways to Peace group, it got easier. I met new friends there, who were trying to change their behavior too. That made it a lot easier.*
>
> *Jeff*

3. List three people, places, and things in your life that could have a good influence on your recovery.

Part Three – Behavioral (Action)

Behavior is action. If an action gives you pleasure, you will want to repeat it. If the action gives you strong pleasure, you may want repeat it over and over no matter what.

Some actions become habits. Habits are created when you repeat certain actions over and over. You created your anger habit by repeating angry behavior. Once a behavior has become a habit, it is very difficult to stop doing that particular behavior. Yet, you can change a behavior that has become a habit. You can change your behavior and break your anger habit.

Recovery from your anger habit must start with changing your angry behavior. But do not wait. Start now to change your angry behavior. If you do not change your behavior now, you will lose more things. You will lose more freedom, more friends, more self-respect.

Eventually you will find it necessary to change in all parts of yourself in order to be happily free of excessive anger. But, first, it is necessary to change your angry behavior. You have already made an Anti-Violence Self-Agreement.

> **MESSAGE FROM PETER**
>
> *My name is Peter. I'm seventeen years old and I have a problem with anger. I wanted to start with finding out how I built my anger habit in the first place. I spent a lot of time looking for answers. Meanwhile, my behavior stayed the same. I needed some skills, some ways to stop myself from acting on my anger and saying things and doing things that get me in trouble. I needed to change my behavior. That's what I had to do first. Finding the causes of my anger could come later.*
>
> *PETER*

SELF-TEST

1. Angry behaviors can become a habit.

   TRUE   FALSE

2. Angry behavior becomes a habit when you repeat the angry behavior over and over.

   TRUE   FALSE

3. You can learn to change your angry behavior and break your anger habit.

TRUE   FALSE

. . . .

Part Four – Skills (Learning)

You were not born with skills, but you were born with the ability to learn skills. Your ability to learn new skills makes it possible to change your angry behavior.

Your skills help you function. They help you obtain things you need or want. You have learned many skills. Now you can learn new skills to deal with things that trigger your anger.

. . . .

SELF-TEST

1. Why do you need skills to recover from your anger habit?

. . . .

Part Five – Values/Goals

Values

MESSAGE FROM SEAN

I had some skills. I'd learned good writing skills–don't make me try to do algebra problems, please don't do that to me! But I can write. I learned some karate skills, too. My sensei said so. I learned these skills by practicing them over and over, and by practicing some more. But I didn't know how to deal with my feelings. I didn't have those kinds of skills. I didn't know how to deal with embarrassment and anxiety and other negative feelings, except to get angry. In fact, anger was the only skill I had when it came to my feelings. And, in a way, anger is a skill. It's something I learned by practicing my angry behavior over and over. The problem is, it's a negative skill. When you use anger to deal with negative feelings, you lose things.

Sean

Values and goals are closely related. Values are the things and feelings that are important to you. Values tell you what will give you pleasure, and they tell you what will bring you pain. Values tell you what to move toward and what to move away from. Values also tell you what to think about. Values have a strong effect on your behavior. Your values even determine what skills you develop. They directly determine your goals. Your values have a strong effect on every other recovery level.

Full recovery from your anger habit requires you to look closely at your values. You will find you will need to change some of your values in order to recover from your anger problem. You will learn more about values later in the workbook.

Goals

Goals are plans for getting the things you want to have and want to do. Goals are plans for the future. You set goals in order to obtain things that will cause you to feel the pleasure of your valued feelings. Goals reinforce your skills and help you make sense of your behavior. Your goals can even affect your body. Full recovery from your anger habit depends, in part, on your goals.

Goals and values give you reasons to keep growing and changing. They give you something to look forward to, and they give you hope. You will learn more about goals later in the workbook.

· ·

SELF-TEST

1. Your values do not have a strong effect on your behavior.

    TRUE   FALSE

2. Full recovery from your anger problem requires you to take a good look at your values.

    TRUE   FALSE

3. Goals are plans for getting what you want and need.

    TRUE   FALSE

4. Goals and values give you certain things (circle the correct answers):

    Reasons to keep growing and changing

    Something to look forward to

    Hope

· ·

Part Six – Beliefs

Your beliefs are one of the most powerful forces in your life. Beliefs are strong feelings; they are not facts. Beliefs are strong feelings about what you think is true or false or right or wrong.

You are not born with your beliefs. You learn your beliefs. You learn your beliefs in a variety of ways. You learn some of your beliefs from other people, from your parents, from friends, and from teachers. You learn some of your beliefs from television, some from books, and some from movies. Also, you learn some of your beliefs from the words of the music you listen to. You learn some of your beliefs from things that happen to you.

You have learned beliefs about yourself and about other people, and you have learned beliefs about the world. You have learned beliefs that are positive and you have learned beliefs that are negative.

Your beliefs will have a powerful influence on whether you overcome your anger habit. Your beliefs give you the energy and the will to change. Your beliefs deeply influence every other part of your whole self, and all other parts influence your beliefs.

In another part of the workbook, you will learn more about beliefs. You will learn the difference between recovery beliefs and beliefs that keep you stuck. You will learn to become aware of your beliefs and you will learn the difference between positive and negative beliefs. You will learn how to change negative beliefs that limit you into positive beliefs that support your recovery from your anger habit.

. . . .

SELF-TEST

1. Look at the statement about beliefs and circle the correct statements.

    You are born with your beliefs.

    You learn your beliefs.

    Beliefs are facts.

    Beliefs are strong feelings.

2. Some beliefs are positive and some beliefs are _____.

3. In order to recover from your anger habit, you will need to change your negative beliefs into positive beliefs.

    TRUE   FALSE

. . . .

Part Seven – Mission (Your Identity)

A complete identity includes a personal mission statement. Your mission statement is a description of what you believe to be your life purpose. Your personal mission, or life purpose, is your reason for living. It is your reason for doing and learning things, and for acquiring things. It is your reason for believing what you believe. In short, it is your reason for being.

Awareness of your personal mission will help you make sense out of everything else. It will help you stay focused on your main goal: to recover from your anger habit. By the way, you are not too young to think about your mission statement.

Successful, non-violent, happy people have a conscious awareness of their personal mission. They believe they have a purpose, and they have a clear idea of what they should be doing with their lives. They feel they know why they are on the earth, and they feel they have a mission to fulfill which will benefit others as well as themselves.

In a special part of the workbook, you will learn more about your mission. You will learn how to write your mission down, so that you can use it to help you recover from your anger habit.

· ·

SELF-TEST

1.   (Fill in the blanks) Your mission statement is a description of what you believe to be your _____.

2.   Your mission, or life purpose, is your reason for living.

TRUE   FALSE

3.   Non-violent happy people have a conscious awareness of their personal mission.

TRUE   FALSE

· ·

Part Eight – Spiritual

You have a spiritual part, whether you know it or not. All people have a spiritual part. It is the part that helps you feel connected in a positive way to other people, to the universe, and to the higher power of your understanding. That is what is meant by the word "spiritual." Used in this way, it does not mean "religious." Your religion is the way you have chosen to express your spiritual part. Your religion is your business. Pathways to Peace wants only to make it clear that all human beings have a part of the self that can be called the spiritual part. If you are an atheist, one who doesn't believe in the existence of a higher power, you have chosen atheism as a way to express your spiritual part. That, too, is your business. If you are an agnostic, one who isn't sure one way or the other, and have chosen agnosticism to express your spiritual part, that is also your business. The point is, if you feel spiritually connected you may discover a purpose which is even bigger than your personal mission. To fully recover and heal from your anger habit, you will need to pay attention to your spiritual part.

Of all the parts of the self, perhaps the spiritual part seems to have the most power. When you develop a spiritual identity it can, and often does, generate revolutionary change in all other parts of the self. Revolutionary change is big change. When you change at the spiritual level, the change may lead to an overall transformation of all other recovery parts. In fact, when change takes place at the spiritual part of the self, the rest of the self must change. Dramatic personal change is almost always triggered by major change at the spiritual level.

> ## MESSAGE FROM JAMES
>
> *I live in Los Angeles. My name is James. I have a problem with anger, and I am sixteen. My mother was a fundamentalist. She was also mentally ill. Her mental illness caused her to interpret her religion in strange ways. She beat me when I was small. She said she did it to get the devil out of me. She said God told her to do it. She'd beat me, then she'd read the Bible to me. When I was twelve they sent my mother to an asylum. I was really angry with God. Then I got hooked on violence. Anger and rage became my god. I got in trouble and had a lot of consequences. Finally, I stopped my violence. But I wasn't happy. My Pathways to Peace mentor told me I had to be non-violent and happy, not just non-violent. My mentor said I had to get spiritually connected. He said if I didn't, I wouldn't be happy. Then I would relapse back into violence, my drug of choice. So I started to open up to my spiritual part. I read about different religions. I'm still exploring, but I think I'm starting to form a healthy relationship with the God of my understanding. I'm starting to feel connected. The only time I ever felt connected before was when I was drunk or high on alcohol and meth.*
>
> *James*

SELF-TEST

1. Your spiritual part helps you feel connected to other people.

    TRUE   FALSE

2. The word "spiritual" means "religious."

    TRUE   FALSE

3. (Fill in the blank.) Dramatic personal change is almost always triggered by change at _____ level.

CHAPTER SEVEN

The Eight Steps of the Recovery Process

R ecovery from an anger habit is an eight-step process.

Step One: The Admission

Admit you caused harm and, whenever possible, apologize and make restitution.

First, you did an honest self-assessment. Now you can admit you caused harm, and wherever possible you can apologize to the people you hurt. In some cases you will want to make restitution. That means paying for damage done to someone's property.

Is there ever a time when you shouldn't apologize or make restitution? In some cases, you may not want to approach a person you have hurt after all. If apologizing to someone you have hurt would for any reason cause them more harm, or would cause harm to someone else, then it may not be a good idea to apologize or make restitution.

Because you have harmed people and, in some cases, their property, you may be experiencing feelings of guilt and shame. The people to whom you apologize or make restitution will know you are trying to change, and it might make them change from ill to good the feelings they hold for you. But your primary purpose for apologizing is to help yourself deal with the feelings of guilt and shame. Feelings of guilt and shame are anger triggers. Apologizing to those you hurt can release you from those negative feelings. Then, guilt and shame can no longer act as anger triggers.

Whenever possible, apologize face to face to those you hurt. Of course, sometimes it might be better to apologize by telephone. Sometimes it won't even be possible to apologize or make restitution. The people you harmed may have moved far away. In those cases you could apologize by letter. But you might not want to actually mail the letter. To do so might cause more harm than good. In that case, you could write the letter but not send it. Putting your apology in writing could help you let go of the negative feelings of guilt and shame (remember, your apology is essentially for your benefit). Once you have written the letter, tear it up and throw it away. That way no harm will come to the other person, and you will have accomplished your goal: to rid yourself of the negative feelings brought on by guilt and shame, so that they may no longer trigger your anger.

Do the best you can as you work the Admission step. This step is a process, not something you can do in one sitting. You will want to continue working this step throughout your recovery.

. . . .

SELF-TEST

1. There may be times when you should not apologize or make restitution.

TRUE   FALSE

2. Explain in a few words exactly what it mean to make restitution.

3. Once you have done the Admission step, you will never have to do the step again.

TRUE   FALSE

. . . .

Step Two: Taking Responsibility

*Accept responsibility for your actions, decide
to stop your harmful behavior, and become
willing to forgive others and yourself.*

You did not take responsibility for your actions in the past; instead you blamed others. Now you have learned to "own" your behavior, and "own" the results of your behavior. That means you have decided to take responsibility. It means you have decided to stop blaming others for your anger problem, and to stop blaming them for the consequences you have had to pay for your behavior.

You already completed and signed the Anti-Violence Self-Agreement. Now you are responsible for following through on that agreement. What if you break your agreement? You are now accountable for your behavior. That's what the agreement means. And if you break it, it means you must pick yourself up and get back on the recovery track.

Other people have hurt you. Holding on to these "hurts" keeps you angry. This is called resentment. Also, you have done things which have hurt others and probably feel some guilt and shame. You must get past the resentment, guilt, and shame. You must let go of it. The way to let go is to forgive.

In order to heal from your anger problem, and be happy, you need to become willing to forgive those who harmed you. Also you need to become willing to forgive yourself for the harm you have done to others. To forgive others and yourself will release you from the guilt, shame, and resentment that have kept you stuck in anger. This is not a simple task. And like Step One, it is an ongoing process. In Chapter 18 you will learn more about forgiveness.

· ·

SELF-TEST

1. Holding on to resentment keeps you stuck in anger.

     TRUE   FALSE

2. Describe something you have done that you feel guilt or shame about. What can you do to release yourself from the guilt and shame?

3. Explain in a few words how forgiving people who have hurt you could help your recovery.

. . . .

Step Three: Violence is Never Justified

Come to realize violence is never justified.

In the past, you used physical or verbal violence in order to feel powerful. You used angry behavior to try to gain power and control over other people. You used it to try to control situations and things. You tried to justify your violent behavior. You made excuses. You told yourself the victims of your violence deserved what they got.

In the past there were times when you, yourself, were treated badly by other people. They were rude to you. They said things that hurt your feelings. Sometimes other people hurt you, physically. They hit you or shoved you. You responded with anger and rage. You probably called it 'getting even.' You may have said to yourself, 'Vengeance is sweet!' But where does it end? As someone recovering from an anger problem, you are learning other ways to respond when people hurt you. Revenge is a luxury you cannot afford.

You have an anger habit, if not a full-blown addiction to anger. Sometimes you get drunk on anger and rage, the way some people get drunk on beer or whiskey. You end up harming others. Then you end up having to pay dues. That means you end up losing something; something gets taken away from you, such as your freedom. As someone with an anger problem, can you ever justify violence? The answer should be a loud "NO!"

It is time to put all arguments aside. Some people may think violence is justified. Maybe they can afford to think so. But in good conscience, you cannot. Not as a person who has an anger habit. It is time to commit yourself to the belief that violence in any form is never justified.

. . . .

SELF-TEST

1. As a person with an anger problem, revenge is a luxury you cannot afford.

TRUE   FALSE

2. List two times you used physical or verbal violence to feel powerful, and felt justified.

3. As a person with an anger problem, violence is never justified.

TRUE   FALSE

. . . .

Step Four: Learn New Ways to Feel Powerful

> *Learn ways to feel personal power without violating other people's right to feel safe in their person and property.*

You have learned that anger made you feel powerful. You probably learned it at an early age. Now you have decided to change. Your angry behavior has harmed others. It has harmed property. Now you have decided to stop using anger and violence as tools of power and control. But in order to stop the old angry behavior, and keep it stopped, you will need to learn new skills. You must learn new ways to change how you feel, new ways to feel powerful. Throughout the rest of this workbook, you will learn new ways to feel powerful that do not threaten other people's right to feel safe.

. . . .

SELF-TEST

1. How old were you when you learned that anger made you feel powerful?

    I was _____ years old when I learned anger made me feel powerful.

2. In order to stop your angry behavior, you will need to learn new skills.

TRUE   FALSE

. . . .

Step Five: Treat People and Property With Respect

Treat all people and their property with the respect and dignity that you, yourself, deserve and expect.

Your angry behavior harmed others, and you may have been harmed by other people. Besides hurting you physically, other people may have injured your sense of self-respect and personal dignity. As a result, you may have felt worthless. Then you may have used anger and rage to make others feel worthless too. You may have taken your revenge out on people who had never harmed you in any way. You may have robbed others of their self-respect and dignity, the way these things had been taken away from you. But now you are beginning see that the people you hurt really didn't deserve the pain you caused them, and now you want to stop hurting other people. So you need to make yourself a promise. You need to promise yourself you will treat others with the respect and dignity that you, yourself, deserve and expect. You need to do so, no matter what has been done to you. No matter how others may have hurt you.

• •

SELF-TEST

1. Did your angry behavior harm others?

   YES   NO

2. Were you ever hurt by other people?

   YES   NO

3. In a few words, describe an incident when someone robbed you of your respect and dignity?

• •

Step Six: Change Negative Beliefs to Positive Beliefs

Let go of negative beliefs, and adopt positive beliefs about yourself, other people, and the world.

You probably have many negative beliefs. Negative beliefs support your anger habit and keep you stuck in angry behavior. Step Six asks you to identify the beliefs that have kept you stuck, and then let go of them. Then Step Six asks you to adopt positive beliefs that will support non-violence and help you change your angry behavior. You will learn more about beliefs in Chapter 15.

· ·

SELF-TEST

1. Negative beliefs support your anger habit.

TRUE   FALSE

2. Step Six asks you to let go of negative beliefs and adopt positive beliefs about yourself, other people, and the world.

TRUE   FALSE

· ·

Step Seven: Believe You Can Change, Find Your Purpose

Come to believe you can change and grow, and that you have a special purpose to fulfill.

You can change and grow. But if you believe you can't change and grow, then you will be unable to change and grow. In order to recover and heal from your anger habit, you will need to adopt the belief that you can change and grow.

You may not believe that your life has a purpose, but Step Seven asks you to adopt the belief that your life does have a purpose—a very special purpose. The belief that your life has a purpose is one of the keys to personal change and growth. If you believe you have a special purpose for being alive, you will have a reason to change—a big reason. And you will have hope. You have a big change to make, and you must have a big reason to make the change. You can find that big reason in your life purpose.

· ·

SELF-TEST

1. You can change and grow, if you believe you can.

TRUE   FALSE

2. Step Seven asks you to adopt the belief that your life has a special purpose.

TRUE   FALSE

. . . .

Step Eight: Transformation

Continue your path of emotional, mental, and spiritual growth. Forgive others and yourself. Help other angry people find their pathway to peace.

Recovery from an anger problem is an ongoing process. Step Eight urges you to continue your personal program of emotional, mental, and spiritual growth. If you continue to work hard, positive changes will happen. Not only will your behavior change. Your attitude will change, your outlook will change, your character will change in a major way. You will be transformed. You will find joy in helping others recover from anger and rage.

. . . .

SELF-TEST

1. Recovery from an anger problem is an ongoing process.

TRUE   FALSE

2. Explain in a few words what will happen if you continue to work hard on changing yourself.

. . . .

MESSAGE FROM SEAN

Here I am again—Sean. When I started following these eight steps, I noticed my behavior started changing. I was feeling better about myself and other people, too. I was feeling better about the world. I was starting to think maybe the stupid leaders of the world weren't going to blow us all up after all. My mood was better, and I knew it was because I was following the Eight Steps of the Pathways to Peace program. Then I knew it was time to start helping other teens who had anger problems. First I did it because I felt like I had to. Now I do what I can to help other teens because I want to. And, you know what? It makes me feel good about myself.

Sean

CHAPTER EIGHT

Motivate Yourself to Change

In this chapter you will learn a method that will increase your desire to stop using violence, and to recover from your anger habit. It is a self-motivation method.

The motivation method you will learn is based on the story, *A Christmas Carol*, by Charles Dickens. You may have seen the movie, or you may have read the book. The main character was Ebenezer Scrooge.

You may recall that Scrooge was visited by several spirits. One of the spirits took Scrooge back into the past. It showed Scrooge things he had said and done in the past that had harmed others, and it showed him things that he had lost because of his behavior.

Another spirit took Scrooge into the future. This spirit showed Scrooge how he would continue to hurt others if he didn't change, and it showed him what other things he would lose if he didn't change how he behaved.

The spirits showed Scrooge he would have to change completely. They showed him he would have to change not only his behavior, but he would have to change his entire character, his whole self. The spirits showed Scrooge he would have to undergo a complete transformation. Otherwise he would continue to lose things and never be happy. The lesson Scrooge learned from the spirits was a painful one. But the lesson also held a light of hope.

The self-motivation method is written in the form of a script. You could simply read the script to yourself, but it would be better to have a friend read it to you while you sit back and listen. If you wish, you could have a counselor read it to you. In either case, you are still the one doing the important work. You will be doing the work using your mind and your imagination.

You need to have a good place in which to read the script or have it read to you. Choose a quiet, comfortable place. Choose a place where you will not be disturbed for at least ten minutes.

The script should be read slowly. The reader should pause after each sentence. Pausing will allow you time to process and personalize the information. The script should be followed as it is written and should be read with feeling. The reading should take no less than ten minutes to allow you to thoroughly process your feelings.

MESSAGE FROM SEAN

I knew about Charles Dickens's book A Christmas Carol, *the story about Ebenezer Scrooge. My mom used to read it to me when I was a little kid. I saw the old movie too, on DVD. Dickens is still one of my favorite old-time writers. Even when I was little, the story about Scrooge sometimes made me stop and think about my life and about my behavior. I'd read the book and watched the video many times over the years. So when I first read the self-motivation script Bill wrote based on this story, it was easy for me to get into. First I read it to myself. It worked pretty good. But then a friend said I'd get a lot more out of it if I let someone else read the script to me. So I let my counselor read it to me. She did a good job, I can tell you. When she got to the end of the first part, I was pretty uncomfortable. I wanted to call it quits. But my counselor encouraged me to let her read the rest to me. She won. I'm glad, too. Because when she finished the second part of the script, I felt like it'd been worth it. My counselor and I spent the next couple of sessions talking about some of the stuff that I remembered and felt, stuff that came out of the first part of the script. But we spent time talking about the good things that came out of the second part too. I read the script again whenever I feel my motivation to change start to get weak. Now here's the script. Bill said for me to read it to you. So listen up.*

Sean

The Motivation Script

Part One

Close your eyes and relax. Think about your anger. Think about the things you've lost because of your anger habit. Think about how much self-respect you've lost. Notice how your anger has wrecked your ability to set and reach goals. Notice what it's done to your freedom. How much guilt and shame are you carrying around, because anger's been running your life for so long? Be aware of the pain, maybe for the first time, that your anger and rage has caused others. C'mon, do yourself a favor. Feel it. Don't be mad at me! I'm just the guy reading the script. It's about you. It's about your thoughts, your memories.

Now remember back to the first loss you suffered because of your anger, whatever it was. Exactly what was that first loss? Did you lose a friend—maybe your girlfriend or boyfriend? Was that your first loss? Maybe they kicked you out of school. Was that your first big loss? Did you get sent to a detention center and lose your freedom? Did you lose your self-respect? That's what a lot of people lose first. How did that first loss, whatever it was, make you feel? By the way, did you feel proud of yourself? Or did you feel ashamed?

Now think of all the other things you lost because of your anger. Start with that first loss, way back when. Then think of all the other things you've lost since that time, right up to the present. Think about all those other losses, one by one. Take your time. Now let yourself get in touch with how those losses made you feel. Get in touch with the pain. People talked about Scrooge behind his back. They said real mean things about Scrooge. What do you think people were saying about you behind your back?

Now, like Scrooge in the story, travel into the future. Go one year into the future, and imagine you're still using anger and violence like a drug to change how you feel. But before you go, you have to pick up all the things you've lost and all the pain, and take them with you. Cram all that stuff down inside a huge bag. Like a huge book bag, that you could practically cram a car in. Now throw that huge bag of pain over your shoulder, and tighten the straps, and carry it into the future with you. Makes a heavy load, doesn't it? All those losses and all that pain weigh you down, huh? Too bad. And every new loss piles on more weight. You're on foot, by the way, not riding in a car or on the subway. Nope, you have to walk. A year has passed. You're still using anger like a drug to change how you feel. How many friends have you lost now? How many weeks, or months, have you spent in detention? What do you think people are saying about you now behind your back? How much worse are things going for you now, after one whole year?

Now trudge on ahead another year—hey, don't forget the bag! You can't leave that behind, for somebody else to carry. It's your stuff. But that bag's really heavy now, after another year of stuffing it full of losses and pain. Come on now, pick it up, throw it on your back. Two years have gone by, and you're still using anger like a drug. What's your life like now? What has anger cost you? How much freedom have you lost? How many friends? Maybe you've lost all your friends by now. If you have, don't be surprised. Is your self-respect totally gone? What do you think people are saying about you behind your back now? You've been using anger and rage like a drug for two more years.

Have you become a drug addict or an alcoholic by now too? Or maybe you had some clean time and then had a relapse because of your anger and rage. Anger's the biggest relapse trigger there is, in case you didn't know. Maybe by now you're not even alive. Right, maybe you're dead from an overdose. Maybe they found your body in an alley somewhere, behind some garbage cans. Is that you lying there, with your eyes bulging out of your head, the needle still sticking out of your arm? Man, I hope not! How many people have you hurt? You've used anger to feel powerful for two more years. Count up your losses. Get in touch with the pain. Now how do you feel about yourself?

(Pause here for at least 60 seconds.)

Part Two

In your imagination come on back to the present. Set the bag down and rest for a minutes. Like Scrooge, take a breather. You can open your eyes if you want.

Okay. Close your eyes again and get ready to do some more time-traveling, back to the future—but wait a minute! Don't forget the bag. You can't take a walk into the future without that. Remember, it's your stuff. But as you pick up the bag and hoist it on your back, it feels different, doesn't it? Lighter, maybe? Yeah, a lot lighter. That's because you dumped a lot of junk out of the bag. A lot of guilt, a lot of shame, maybe a lot of detention time—a lot of losses. And it was those losses that made the bag so heavy. Yep, you've dumped a bunch of things out of the bag.

So now in your imagination, see yourself another whole year in the future. But this time you've stopped using anger like a drug to change how you feel. You haven't done anything violent for a whole year! You've stopped hurting people with words and actions. You don't break things anymore. You don't threaten people. You're not perfect—nobody is. Sure, you still get angry once in a while. You're human! But you've stopped doing the things you used to do that got you in so much trouble and made you lose so many things. You've learned how to manage your anger. You've stopped the violence and you've learned new ways to respond to old triggers. You've been working a recovery program for your anger problem for a whole year.

You've been rage-free for a whole year. How've you benefited? What's your life like now? What've you gained by changing your behavior? How have you benefited from working a recovery program for a whole year? How many friends do you have now? And what about your self-respect? How do you feel about yourself now? Because you've been rage-free for a whole year, what have you been able to accomplish? What do you think people are saying about you now?

Now go two more years into the future. Carry all the benefits with you, instead of all that pain and all those losses. The bag's getting lighter all the time, isn't it? Get in touch with how you feel about yourself because you've changed. In your imagination, listen to the good things people say about you. See yourself happy and content, respected and loved, and accomplishing your goals. See yourself at peace with yourself and the world.

(Pause here for 60 seconds.)

Now come back to the present again. Don't open your eyes yet. But come back to the present. It's time to make a choice. It's the most important choice you'll ever make. It's the most important choice anybody could ever make. Are you ready? Take it from me, Sean, you're as ready as you'll ever be. Take a minute to think about both parts of the Motivation Script. Think about yourself. Be serious now. Don't make a mistake and choose the wrong thing. Be very careful. You see, what you have to choose—is your future. Each part of the Motivation Script led to the future. But each part led to a different kind of future. The first part of the script led to a future filled with losses and pain. Remember? The second part led to a future anybody would want to live in. Right?

Now, take a deep breath and focus. Now—choose! Choose the kind of future you want for yourself. Choose right now, you don't have any more time!

(Pause here for 60 seconds.)

Now sit quietly and let your mind process what you've just done. Let your mind process the thoughts and memories. Let your body process the feelings. Spend at least five minutes processing.

When I went through this with my counselor, I felt like I'd run about a hundred miles without a break. I was still thinking about it the next day. Mostly, I was thinking about Part One of the script. The bad part. I called my counselor, and she said to focus my thinking on Part Two of the script, not Part One. If you're still thinking about Part One the next day, try thinking about Part Two instead.

You will want to use this method more than once. Repeat the method any time you notice a decrease in your motivation to change your behavior. Allow a day or two to pass. Then come back to this chapter and complete the self-test on the next page.

SELF-TEST

1. Describe how you felt after you finished Part One of the Motivation Script.

2. Describe how you felt after reading Part Two of the Motivation Script.

3. What was the choice you made at the end of Part Two?

4. The script asks you to remember the first thing you lost because of anger. Write down what it was you lost.

5. People said negative things about Scrooge behind his back. Write down what you think people were saying about you behind your back.

6. Write down what you think you will lose in the future if you do not recover from your anger habit.

7. Write down how you think you will benefit if you continue your recovery from anger.

8. What kinds of things would you like people to say about you?

CHAPTER NINE

Understand the Anger Process Through the Niagara Falls Metaphor

What is the Niagara Falls Metaphor?

A metaphor is a comparison. The Niagara Falls Metaphor compares anger and rage to a trip down the Niagara River and over the Niagara Falls.

Practically everyone knows about the Niagara River and Niagara Falls. People from all over the world have visited the Falls. If you have not visited Niagara Falls, you have probably seen it in movies. It is one of the Seven Wonders of the World. It is one of the most awesome natural sights a human being could ever see.

The power of the Falls is almost beyond belief. The volume of water that goes over the Falls also stretches the imagination. Water pours over the Falls at the rate of 203,000 gallons per second! But just a few miles upstream from the Falls, the river moves slowly in its channel. People fish from boats in that part of the river. You can't even see or hear the Falls from there. If you were fishing from a boat in that part of the Niagara River you would be safe. Of course your boat would have an engine and a pair of oars, so you would have some control over your boat.

But what would happen if your engine failed and you lost your oars overboard? You would be in deep trouble! You would no longer have control over your boat. You would be at the mercy of the current! The current would carry you toward the

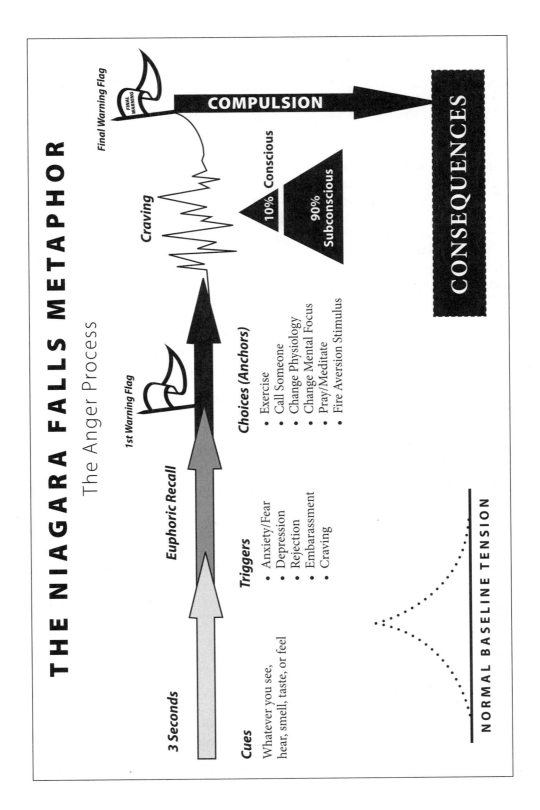

THE NIAGARA FALLS METAPHOR
The Anger Process

3 Seconds

Euphoric Recall

1st Warning Flag

Craving

Final Warning Flag

FINAL WARNING

COMPULSION

CONSEQUENCES

10% Conscious

90% Subconscious

Cues

Whatever you see,
hear, smell, taste, or feel

Triggers
- Anxiety/Fear
- Depression
- Rejection
- Embarrassment
- Craving

Choices (Anchors)
- Exercise
- Call Someone
- Change Physiology
- Change Mental Focus
- Pray/Meditate
- Fire Aversion Stimulus

NORMAL BASELINE TENSION

Falls at an ever increasing rate of speed. The Niagara River moves faster and faster, the closer it gets to the Falls. The power and tension of the river increases.

If you yelled for help at that point, someone might hear you and respond. You could be saved from going over the Falls. Another boat could reach you and tow you and your boat to shore. Or a helicopter could drop a line and pluck you out of the river.

But a hundred yards or so from the brink of the Falls, the river becomes a rushing torrent. If you weren't saved before you got to that point, all would be lost. No one could overcome the power of the river at that point. In order to avoid injury or death you would have to find a way to get out of the river before then. That part of the Niagara River is called the "point of no return."

People who fish in the Niagara River come prepared. Few people lose control and plunge over the Falls to their death. Accidents happen sometimes, but they are rare. Of course, some people have actually chosen to take the plunge over the Falls for glory and fame. They used all kinds of ways, even wrapping themselves in rubber tires. But it is a 160-foot plunge to the bottom of the gorge. Hitting water from that height is like diving from the top of an eight-story building onto concrete. And the bottom of the gorge is littered with boulders. You can count on the fingers of one hand the number of people who have survived a plunge over the Falls. A few people have even used the Falls to commit suicide.

. . . .

SELF-TEST

1. In a few words, describe what the word "metaphor" means.

. . . .

The Niagara Falls Metaphor

According to the Niagara Falls Metaphor, when you are angry it is like ending up in a small boat in the Niagara River, except that your boat is without engine and oars, so you and your boat are under the river's control.

When you get angry, you hurt people, animals, or things, or you say things that you later regret. You become verbally abusive or physically violent. When you are abusive or violent, that is like going over Niagara Falls. Someone suffers injury or something is damaged. Then you experience consequences. That means you lose something you value. For example, you lose friends or you lose your freedom.

Also you are not aware of being in the river. That is another part of the metaphor. That is a scary thought, but it is true. You use anger like a drug and have developed an anger habit. You may, in fact, have developed an addiction to anger. When you have a habit or are addicted to something, you are often not aware of the behavior connected with your habit or addiction. You are not aware when you are in the process of the habit or addiction. In this chapter you will learn how to be aware when you are in the river and in the process called anger and rage. In the next chapter you will learn how to stop the process and get out of the river.

. . . .

SELF-TEST

1. How is getting angry like being in the Niagara River?

2. Part of the metaphor talks about "going over the Falls." Explain in a few words what it means to "go over the Falls"?

. . . .

The Five Stages of the Anger Process

Stage One: Cues and Triggers (Feelings)—Plunging into the River

Anger cues can be people, places, or things. Cues are things you can see or hear. A person you see on the street could be an anger cue. The sound of a person's voice could be a cue. Some cues are things you remember. The memory of a person's face, for example, could be a cue. The memory of a person's voice or the words they said could be a cue. Sometimes you can avoid cues, but most of the time you will have little control over cues that happen. It is the "stuff" of life that happens and which is often beyond your control. The good news is that you can learn how to control memory cues and you can learn how to deal with cues you cannot avoid. The key word is "learn."

Cues connect to feelings. Cues lead to bad feelings or good feelings. Bad feelings are negative, good feelings are positive. Whether a cue leads to a bad feeling or a good feeling depends on how you think about the cue. If you think of the cue as painful, it will cause you to have a bad feeling. If you think of the cue as pleasurable it will cause you to have a good feeling. The bad feelings caused by cues are the triggers for anger and rage.

Anger triggers are always bad feelings. Feelings like fear or frustration are typical anger triggers, because they are painful feelings. They are the kinds of triggers (bad feelings) that plunge you into the river. Triggers (bad feelings) cause your tension level to increase. You have tension in your body all the time because you are alive. It is called baseline tension. Baseline tension is normal tension. But when a cue leads to a bad feeling, such as fear, it causes your tension to go up above what is normal for you. It causes your tension to go above your baseline.

Cues are happening all the time. When a cue is painful, it leads to a bad feeling. Then the bad feeling becomes an anger trigger. The anger trigger (a bad feeling like fear) increases your tension level, causing the level to rise up above normal. The increased tension is what causes you to end up in the anger process. To use the metaphor, it is what causes you to end up in the Niagara River in a small boat without engine or oars.

As soon as you become aware of a trigger you should think: "I have only three seconds to get out of here!" If you assume you have only three seconds to get out of the anger process, you may have a chance to interrupt the process before it's too late. Before you reach the "point of no return" and plunge over the Falls.

A key to recovery from an anger habit is to learn how to manage the bad feelings that trigger your anger. But you also need to learn how to deal with cues that cause the bad feelings. You will learn how to deal with cues that cause bad feelings in the next chapter.

. . . .

SELF-TEST

1. Name one person, one place, and one thing that you think are cues that lead to your anger triggers.

2. Name the trigger (bad feeling) that each cue connects to.

3. Describe in a few words the difference between a cue and a trigger. Give one example of each.

. . . .

Stage Two - Euphoric Recall (First Red Flag)

Stage Two of the anger process is Euphoric Recall. Euphoric means pleasurable. Recall means to remember. Euphoric Recall is a memory of a time when you used anger and it made you feel good. It made you feel high, and you didn't suffer bad consequences. You didn't get kicked out of school or sent to detention. You didn't get hurt or hurt someone you cared about or loved. You didn't end up suffering some kind of punishment. Instead, you felt rewarded. You felt powerful. Euphoric Recall is a natural part of the anger process.

You were already in the Niagara River before Euphoric Recall happened. Whenever you experience Euphoric Recall, that means you are heading toward the Falls. It also means your tension level has gone up even more. Your tension level automatically increases when you don't do something right away to interrupt an anger trigger. Your increased tension causes Euphoric Recall.

Because it happens automatically, you have no control over Euphoric Recall. Also, you are usually not consciously aware of Euphoric Recall when it happens, but Euphoric Recall causes you to move faster toward the Falls. When you experience Euphoric Recall, your mind begins to anticipate the pleasure you will feel when you act on your anger.

The Niagara River acts much like the anger process. The closer the Niagara River gets to the Falls, the more the tension and speed of the river increase. During Euphoric Recall, your brain remembers a time when you used anger and you got pleasurable results. You felt powerful and you avoided negative results. The anticipation of pleasure and the rise in tension increase your desire to use anger and violence. It pushes you faster and faster toward the "point of no return."

You need to learn to see Euphoric Recall as a big red warning flag. As a warning flag, Euphoric Recall pops up out of the river and loudly says, "You fool! You are in the Niagara River, heading for the Falls!"

. . . .

SELF-TEST

1. *Euphoric* means pleasurable, *recall* means to remember.

TRUE   FALSE

2. You have no control over Euphoric Recall.

TRUE   FALSE

3. Using a few words of your own, explain what Euphoric Recall means.

. . . .

Stage Three – Craving (Second Red Flag)

Stage Three of the anger process is called Craving. A craving is a strong urge. In this case, a craving is a strong urge to behave in an angry way.

The Niagara River, which is a process, never stops and never slows down. What happens to the Niagara River the closer it gets to the Falls? You know the answer to this question. The tension and speed of the river increase. The anger process doesn't stop or slow down either. Your tension keeps increasing, like the river. You move faster and closer to angry behavior. You must quickly do something in order to interrupt the process and get out of the river before it is too late.

When you have a craving to use anger, you are very close to the Falls. The river has picked up speed. Once again, your tension level has increased. The increase in your tension level causes the craving.

It is much harder to fight off a craving. That is why it is so important to get out of the river as soon as possible. The closer you get to the Falls, the harder it is to get out of the river.

Think of Craving as a bigger, brighter red flag—much bigger and brighter than Euphoric Recall. It says, "You fool! Not only are you in the Niagara River heading for the Falls, you are right at the brink! You are in white water!" This is the final warning flag!

During the Craving stage, it is as though two voices start an argument inside your head. It is as though two different people are inside your head yelling at each other. You may not be consciously aware of them, but they are there. The first of the two voices will urge you to do or say something violent. It will say, "Do it! Kick! Hit! Slap! Yell! Do something violent!" That voice takes you into deep denial. It wants you to justify and rationalize. That voice doesn't want you to remember the consequences you experienced when you used anger and rage in the past. It wants you to forget about consequences and think only of the pleasure you might experience by acting on your anger. The other voice urges you not to be violent. It says, "No. Don't!" That voice wants you to avoid violence. It wants you to stop and think. It wants you to remember the consequences you suffered in the past when you used angry behavior. That voice wants you to remember the guilt and remorse you felt because of the pain you caused others. You struggle with trying to decide which voice to listen to. But when you experience a craving to use anger, it means your tension level is very, very high. You will have to make a decision very quickly, because you are so close to the point of no return. You must not give in to the first voice. If you listen to the first voice, you lose. You will go over the Falls.

. . . .

SELF-TEST

1. Stage Three of the anger process is called "Craving."

TRUE   FALSE

2. Where are you in the river when a craving to use anger happens? Circle the right answer.

Way upstream, far from the Falls   Very close to the Falls

3. Circle the correct answer. A craving to use anger is caused by:

Lack of awareness   Increased tension

4. A craving to use anger is the final warning flag.

TRUE   FALSE

5. When you experience a craving to use anger, it is as though two voices start an argument inside your head. The first voice will urge you to do something violent. What will happen if you listen to that voice? Circle the correct answer.

Nothing will happen.   You will go over the Falls.

6. In a few of your own words, explain what the word "craving" means.

. . . .

Stage Four—Compulsion

The Fourth Stage of the anger process is called Compulsion. Up to this point you have had a choice. You have had opportunities to stop yourself from going over the Falls. You had opportunities to interrupt the process because you were consciously aware you were in the river, and you had two strong warnings—two big red flags—that told you danger lay ahead.

But there is a big difference between a craving and a compulsion. When you felt a craving, you still had a choice. As stated, you were still consciously aware that you were in the river.

When you feel a compulsion to do anything, whatever it may be,
it means that you no longer have a choice.

When you have a compulsion to use anger, you no longer have a choice. You have no choice because you are no longer aware you are in the river. When you feel a compulsion, it means you can't stop. It means you are already over the Falls. It means your tension has increased beyond the "point of no return." It means you have lost control. When you feel a compulsion to use anger to change how you feel, to change a feeling of powerlessness into a feeling of power, you no longer have control over your anger. The anger process has taken control of you.

Here is another way to understand a compulsion. The mind is like an iceberg. An iceberg sits low in the water. Only about 10 percent of the iceberg—just the tip—shows above the waterline. The other 90 percent of the iceberg remains underwater, hidden from view. The 10 percent that rides above the waterline represents the conscious mind. The part underwater represents the subconscious mind. Your anger is a habit. You have many other habits besides your anger habit. All are stored in your subconscious mind. Habits are automatic behaviors. Your habits stay down in the subconscious mind until something triggers them into action. It is as though they are asleep there, way down deep in your subconscious mind. But certain things will wake up habits. Things that wake up habits are called triggers. As you recall, anger triggers are certain kinds of feelings. Fear, anxiety, disappointment, embarrassment, and rejection are examples of the kind of feelings that trigger anger.

Your subconscious mind watches for triggers. When a trigger connected to a certain habit occurs, the subconscious mind notices it. Then it wakes up the habit that was asleep in your subconscious mind and causes you to go into action—automatically.

That is how it works with your anger habit. That is what happens when you feel a compulsion to act in an angry way. Your tension level increases because you haven't done anything to stop the anger process. You have let your tension level continues to rise. Finally it rises above the point where you can stop it, above the point of no return. That's when you feel a compulsion.

When you feel a compulsion your conscious mind stops functioning, and your subconscious mind takes over. That's when you lose control. Unable to stop yourself, you end up going over the Falls. Then you crash down onto the boulders at the bottom of the gorge. In other words, you become angry and you do something or say something that hurts someone or damages their property. Then you suffer consequences.

. . . .

SELF-TEST

1. When you feel a craving to use anger, you still have a choice.

TRUE   FALSE

2. When you feel a compulsion to do anything, you no longer have a _____ (fill in the blank).

3. A compulsion means you still have control of the anger process.

TRUE   FALSE

4. The mind is like an iceberg. The subconscious part of the mind floats above the waterline.

TRUE   FALSE

5. Anger is a habit. Like all habits, your anger is stored in the subconscious part of the mind.

TRUE   FALSE

6. When you reach the Compulsion stage, what or who is in control of the anger process?

. . . .

Stage Five—Consequences (Negative Results)

The Fifth Stage of the anger process is called Consequences. You suffer consequences when you use anger and rage to change how you feel. Consequences are negative results. Losing something you value is a negative result. When you go over the Falls, you cannot avoid losing something you value. You may get kicked out of school and lose your educational opportunities. You may get sent to detention and lose your freedom. You may lose your best friend. Or you may lose your self-respect. Of course, you end up feeling bad instead of good. You end up feeling guilty and ashamed, or embarrassed. The point is, you experience consequences when you use anger and violence.

The guilt, shame, and embarrassment become triggers too. These bad feelings keep you stuck in the process. They send you right back into the river. The process becomes a circulating pump. A cue happens. That is, you see, hear, or remember something that leads to a bad feeling. The bad feeling triggers your anger. You plunge into the river and harm someone or something. Then you go over the Falls and crash down onto the rocky gorge. You lose something you value, and feel guilty and ashamed. Then the guilt and shame circulate back through the process. Pretty soon you think you must be crazy. But there is a way out. You can change. The next chapter will help you learn how.

· ·

SELF-TEST

1. Write down three consequences you have had because of your anger.

2. In your own words, describe the "circulating pump" effect of guilt and shame.

3. Name the five stages of the anger process.

    Stage One: _____

    Stage Two: _____

> **MESSAGE FROM JULIO**
>
> *I'm Julio. I live in Texas and I've got a big anger problem. I'm in the 9th grade. I've never been to the Niagara Falls, but I know about rivers and I know about waterfalls. I have lived near the Rio Grande River ever since I moved here from Mexico with my father and mother, when I was three years old. Comparing anger to the Niagara Falls helps me understand my anger problem better than anything else. It helps me know when I'm in the anger process, and it helps me know where I am in the process and what I need to do to get out of it. I use the Niagara Falls metaphor to help me stay aware of the anger process. I can say to myself, 'I'm starting to get angry. I'm in the river. What part am I in? What do I need to do to get out?' Knowing about the metaphor I am able to get out of my anger quick enough to avoid more consequences.*
>
> *Julio*

Stage Three: _____

Stage Four: _____

Stage Five: _____

· ·

CHAPTER TEN

Basic Ways to Interrupt the Anger Process

Overview of How You Learned Your Anger Habit

You learned your anger habit by repeating angry behavior over and over in response to certain feelings (triggers). Your anger became a habit, an automatic behavior. Your anger habit is an automatic behavior which is now permanently stored in your subconscious mind. Your subconscious mind includes all the habits you have learned. It also includes your instincts. The instinct to breathe is stored in your subconscious mind. You do not have to learn instincts. You are born with them.

When your angry behavior became a habit, you began to respond automatically with anger whenever your brain noticed one of your anger triggers. Your subconscious mind took over the operation of your anger habit. Therefore, you lost control of the anger process. From then on, you found yourself doing or saying angry things even when you didn't want to do or say angry things.

But you can learn new ways to respond to the same old anger triggers. You can learn new behaviors. And then you can decide to make different choices based on the new behaviors you learn and then you can learn to repeat the new behaviors over and over in response to the old anger triggers. The old triggers will not change or go away. They will still be there in your environment and in your thoughts. But you will learn different ways to respond when the old triggers happen. Instead of responding by saying or doing angry things, you will say or do different things. Notice how much the process of learning different ways to respond to old anger triggers is like the process you used in order to learn your angry behavior. But there is one major difference: you learned your anger program using the unconscious part of your mind. You will learn your recovery program using the conscious part of your mind. Therefore, you will be the one in charge. You will consciously create your own plan of recovery from excessive anger.

Learning new behaviors and then learning to repeat the new behaviors instead of the old angry behaviors when anger triggers occur are the beginning of recovery from your anger habit. It is the beginning of your pathway to peace. Finally the new behaviors will become a new habit, a new set of automatic behaviors. You will acquire a new habit called recovery. Then your subconscious mind will take over the operation of the recovery process. It will become automatic.

Will You Ever Forget Your Anger Habit?

You will never forget your anger habit. Once a behavior becomes a habit, your brain cannot forget it. Habits are stored in brain cells. So you will never forget how to use anger and violence to change how you feel.

Consider the skills for riding a bicycle. Your bicycle skills are a set of behaviors that you practiced over and over until they become a habit. Your bicycle skills are stored in your subconscious mind. Will you ever forget how to ride a bicycle? No.

You will never forget how to use anger to change how you feel. No matter how many new ways you learn to respond differently to anger triggers, your old automatic anger program will sometimes try to take over again. This will be especially true in the beginning, when you first start to practice different ways to respond to anger triggers. But the more you practice the new ways, the less the old angry ways will try to take over. Your recovery program will become

> **MESSAGE FROM DAVID**
>
> *My name is Dave. I'm from New York City. I go to high school. I was working a good anger recovery program. I learned some new skills, and I was handling triggers better than ever. I hadn't been in trouble in more than three months. Then I stopped focusing on my program as much. I stopped doing some of the things that I had learned. I wish I hadn't. I started to think I had it made, that I didn't have to think about my recovery anymore. I forgot that I had an anger habit. About two weeks later, somebody said something—it doesn't matter what. What the person said made me feel embarrassed, and embarrassment is one of my major triggers. I dove into the river. Before I knew it, I was too far downstream. I got angry with the person. He was my boss where I had a part-time job after school. I didn't attack him or break anything. I shouted at him and swore. Bottom line is, I lost my job. Man, I needed that job! I found out I hadn't forgotten how to use anger to change how I feel.*
>
> *David*

stronger and stronger. Finally, after a lot of practice, your recovery program will become stronger, by far, than your old anger program. Then you will find yourself responding to old triggers using one of your new ways. Your recovery program will have become automatic.

Because you are a human being you will end up in the anger process from time to time, no matter how hard you try to avoid it. But you can learn how to interrupt the anger process and get out of it, out of the river, before you go over the Falls. In other words, you can learn new behaviors, new ways to respond to anger triggers. Once you learn some new behaviors, then you will have the power to choose how you will respond to triggers. You now know that if you continue your old angry behavior, you will continue to experience consequences. You will learn many more choices later in the workbook.

When you are the one in charge, you may also choose to stay in the anger process. If you choose to stay in the process, even though you now know how it works, then your tension will continue to increase. Finally your old anger habit will take control again. You will feel a compulsion, and your anger habit will escape from your subconscious mind like a raging beast from its cage. You will plunge over the Falls again, because you will no longer have a choice.

· ·

SELF-TEST

1. You learned your anger habit by repeating angry behavior over and over.

TRUE   FALSE

2. Why will you never be able to "forget" your anger habit?

· ·

Three Steps to Interrupt the Anger Process

Check Your Body

You have learned that you are not consciously aware when your anger habit gets triggered. A trigger occurs, and you don't notice it. That is because your subconscious mind operates your anger habit. Your subconscious mind notices the trigger, but it doesn't let your conscious mind know. So you are not aware of the trigger.

Remember the metaphor? Anger is like the Niagara River and Niagara Falls. If you are not aware you are in the river, you will not be able to get out in time. You will go over the Falls. Therefore, you will need to learn how to be aware when you are in the river. You will need to learn to be aware you are in the river, as soon as a trigger occurs, because the trigger is the first step of your anger habit. The trigger is what causes you to plunge into the river. So the first step to getting out of the river is to have a way of knowing you are in the river.

If you are alive you already have a certain level of tension in your body. It is called baseline tension. That is your normal tension level. When an anger trigger occurs, your tension level suddenly rises. It rises up above your normal tension level. Your tension level spikes. Until now, you have had no conscious control over the increased tension. When your tension suddenly rises, it is like what happens when you sit down and cross your legs and tap that certain spot under your knee cap. When you tap that spot, your lower leg automatically jumps. It is sometimes called the knee-jerk response. It is a reflex. When an anger trigger occurs, your tension level responds in a similar way. It jumps higher automatically.

Although your mind will not know, your body will know immediately when an anger trigger occurs. Your body will then immediately send your mind the message that your tension level has increased. But your body sends the message to the subconscious part of your mind. The mind is like an iceberg, remember? The subconscious part of the mind is below the waterline and is hidden from the conscious part of your mind. So the conscious part of your mind has, in the past, been unable to notice the message. But you can learn how to get in touch with how your body sends the message.

Your tension will increase more in a certain body area than in another. It is an individual thing. That is, not everybody feels the increased tension in the same body area. So you must first find out where you feel the increased tension in your body. Then you can learn to notice when the tension level in that body area increases. Then you will have an easy way to know when you are in the anger process. Anger triggers are always certain feelings, negative feelings, bad feelings. The trigger that causes your tension level to rise and that leads to angry behavior could be a feeling of fear or it could be a feeling of frustration. It could be anxiety or disappointment. The trigger could be any negative feeling. But you don't have to know what the trigger is. All you have to know is that your tension level has increased.

. . . .

SELF-TEST

1. Baseline tension describes your normal tension level.

TRUE   FALSE

2. Anger triggers cause your baseline tension to rise above normal.

TRUE   FALSE

3. Your body will know when your tension level has increased.

TRUE   FALSE

. . . .

Step One – Finding Out Where Your Body Feels Increased Tension

The first step to interrupt the anger habit is to check your body to find out where your body feels increased tension. Then you will know when you are in the anger process. The method outlined below will help you learn how to find out where you feel increased tension in your body.

Part One:

a. Think of a time you were angry.
b. Pay attention to your body tension.
c. Notice exactly where your body feels the most tension.

Part Two:

When an anger trigger happens, the first place I feel a sudden increase in tension in my body is (check the body area that applies to you):

❑   my stomach

❑   my lower back

❑   my jaws

❑   back of my neck

❑   behind my eyes

❑   other (write down the area) _____

Now you know what body area you feel increased tension in when a trigger happens; now you have a way of knowing when you are in the river. Practice paying attention to that area of your body. You must learn to notice anger triggers as soon as possible, so you will have the best possible chance of getting out of the river in time. If you do not notice triggers right away, your risk of going over the Falls increases. If you do not notice the triggers until you feel a compulsion, remember what will happen? It will be too late. By then you will already be over the Falls.

Step Two – Make a List of Your <u>Triggers, Choices, and Consequences,</u> and Make a List of the <u>Benefits</u> of Changing Your Behavior.

Now you have learned to be consciously aware of the anger triggers which cause increased tension in your body. Now you must learn how to be consciously aware of the rest of the anger process. Now you will learn how to be consciously aware of your choices, and you will learn how to be consciously aware of your consequences (what you will lose if you go over Niagara Falls again). You must also learn to be consciously aware of the benefits of recovering from your anger habit. Until you have learned how to maintain conscious awareness of the process, your anger habit will continue to control you and run your life. You must take back control.

In Step Two, you will make a list of your triggers, your choices, and your consequences, and you will make a list of the benefits of changing your behavior. A special page has been provided at the end of this chapter to complete this lesson.

Important: After you have made your list, it is suggested that you make three copies. Carry one copy of your list in your wallet or purse. Tape a copy of your list to the wall next to the bathroom mirror, or on the wall of your bedroom next to the door. Keep a copy of your list where you read or watch television. You could type your list into your computer. You could record your list on your iPod or MP3 player. Then you could refer to your list even when you are not at home. Look at the list every day, or listen to it on your iPod or MP3 player. Referring to the list will help you stay consciously aware of how your anger habit works. And it will help you stay aware of how you will benefit by changing the behavior.

Triggers

You have learned that anger triggers are always negative feelings, like those listed below. You know your triggers put the anger process in motion, by causing your tension level to rise. Ask yourself: "What are the feelings that trigger my anger?"

Examples of triggers:

- Embarrassment
- Frustration
- Disappointment
- Anxiety

Each of the examples, above, are common anger triggers. Chances are, one or more of the examples apply to you. But there are other triggers that may apply to you which are not listed among the examples above. Probably there are many others. You will want to make sure that you list all of your major triggers, the ones that most often trigger your anger.

Choices

Choices are things you could do instead of responding to anger triggers in the same old destructive way. Below is a brief list of possible choices. Whatever choices you choose to put on your list must be your choices, not someone else's choices. The choices you list must be things you would actually do. Also, you need many choices. You need choices that will work any time, anywhere. You need choices that will work at two o'clock in the afternoon when you are at school. You need choices that will work at two o'clock in the morning when you are home and cannot sleep. You need choices that will work no matter when you are in the river, and no matter where you are in the river. You may be way upstream where the river runs slowly or way downstream where the river runs faster, down closer to the "point of no return."

When you begin to list your choices, ask yourself: "What could I do when a trigger occurs, instead of going over the Falls? What could I do instead of saying or doing an angry thing?" Spend some time on this step to interrupt the anger process. Think of as many choices as you can, and write them down on the page provided at the end of this chapter.

Examples of choices:

- Call someone on the phone
- Exercise
- Listen to a relaxing CD
- Watch a funny DVD

Later in the workbook you will learn other new choices. Be sure to add them to your list.

Consequences

Going over the Falls means acting out your anger. It means behaving in an angry way. Yelling, name calling, hitting, or injuring yourself—these are examples of going over the Falls. Whenever you go over the Falls, you or other people suffer the consequences of your actions. Your actions hurt people physically or mentally or emotionally. Your actions cause pain. When you act out in anger and hurt yourself or other people, you end up with consequences too. You lose something you value. No one goes over Niagara Falls without suffering consequences. The list below is just to help you get started on Step Three of interrupting the anger process. When you make your list, get in touch with how you will feel if you suffer the losses on your list.

What do you think you might lose if you go over Niagara Falls again? Will you end up in a detention center this time? Will you end up in prison, maybe for 20 years, because you killed someone in a fit of rage? Will you end up with a permanent injury? What will you lose? To get started, ask yourself this question: What will I lose if I go over Niagara Falls again? Pay attention to how the losses make you feel.

Examples of consequences:

- Loss of friends
- Loss of freedom
- Loss of education
- Loss of self-respect

Benefits of Changing Your Angry Behavior

It is hard to change any behavior that has become a habit. You have learned that you have an anger habit. Knowing what you will lose if you don't change your angry behavior is important. But knowing how you will benefit if you do change your angry behavior is also important. If you cannot see a benefit it will be harder to change your behavior, and it will be harder to keep the behavior changed. To benefit means to have good things happen to you. A benefit is the opposite of a consequence. Ask yourself: "How will I benefit by stopping my angry behavior?"

Examples of benefits:

- More friends
- More personal freedom
- More peace of mind
- Able to finish school
- Feel better about yourself

Making a list of your anger triggers, your choices, and your consequences, and making a list of the benefits if you change your angry behavior are very important. The lists on the page at the end of this chapter will help you to recover from your anger problem.

· ·

SELF-TEST

1. Explain in a few words why it will be useful to make a list of your triggers, your choices, and your consequences, as well as a list of the benefits of changing your angry behavior?

· ·

Step Three—Exercise Your New Choices (the Action Step)

Step Three is the Action Step. It is another important part of the recovery process. This step requires you to do something. Think of each new choice as an anchor in the bottom of your boat. Each anchor has a different length of rope attached. When a trigger occurs you must throw an anchor toward shore and hold onto the end of the rope. The anchor must sink into the riverbank on the other side of the river. Then, holding onto the rope you must pull yourself out of the river. Notice the key word: YOU.

At first, your new program will seem strange and uncomfortable. You may find some of your new choices may not work as well as you thought they would. If so, it is okay to change them or add new ones. The same is true of triggers, consequences, and benefits. Change and add to your list when you need to. Your recovery program, like you, is a work in progress. The secret to your success is to keep working on changing your angry behavior.

Any program of recovery must be self-initiated and self-maintained. That means you have to be the one in charge. It means you have to be the one who decides and the one who acts. That is how recovery works.

Although you must not rely on someone else to save you, it is also very important to reach out for help whenever you need it. In fact, you should ask for help wherever and whenever possible. Attending Pathways to Peace meetings can provide the kind of help you need (you will learn more about Pathways to Peace later in the workbook). Surround yourself with friends who want you to succeed. Let them be your cheerleaders. Talking with a counselor can help. Yet you must be in charge of your own recovery. You must take charge of the process. You are the one who is responsible for your recovery. You run the show.

> **MESSAGE FROM SEAN**
>
> *Hi. Sean, again. I knew I needed a way to understand my anger habit and needed a way to stay consciously aware of how my anger habit worked. For me, it had to be easy to learn and easy to remember. The Niagara Falls Metaphor is just what I needed. At first, I didn't want to do any work. I thought I could slide by without making lists, and all that. Finally, I went ahead and did what the guidebook suggested. I made a list of my anger triggers, my choices, and my consequences. Then I made a list of the benefits I'd get if I changed my angry behavior, and kept it changed. Making the lists definitely helped. I even made copies and stuck them around the house where every day I'd see what I wrote down. I recorded my list on my MP3 player and listened to them when I had time. After a while I didn't have to look at the list. You see, I've had it! I don't want to hurt anybody anymore, and I sure don't want to pay any more consequences–damn!*
>
> *SEAN*

• •

SELF-TEST

1. Step Three to interrupt the anger process is the Action Step. What does Step Three tell you to do?

2. Any recovery program, in order to be successful, must be self-initiated and self-maintained. Explain in a few words what that means.

. . . .

My Triggers...

My Choices...

The Consequences of My Anger...

The Benefits of Changing My Behavior...

PART THREE

Changing Your Behavior

CHAPTER ELEVEN

Your Physical Needs as Part of the Recovery Process

Nutrition

How you take care of your body has a great deal to do with how you feel. Nutrition has a direct effect on the biological (physical) part of recovery from an anger habit. Nutrition has an indirect effect on all other parts of your whole self, proving once again the importance of balance.

Poor nutrition has a negative effect on your ability to manage anger. A diet high in sugar, for example, can lead to mood swings that may intensify anger triggers. You need a well-balanced diet which is low in sugar. You need plenty of protein. Ideally you should eat a variety of foods, including plenty of fresh fruits and vegetables. Try new fruits and vegetables. They add texture, color, taste, and interest. They also add vitamins and make eating and preparing food more fun.

Use of caffeine increases you body's tension level and makes it harder to control your anger. Use it sparingly. Use of alcohol, tobacco, and other non-prescribed drugs also has a negative effect. Do not use them. You will learn more about the negative effects of drugs later in the workbook.

You need to take in nutritious food at regular meals. Going long periods (more than five or six hours) without eating a regular meal makes you more sensitive to anger triggers. Pay attention to your diet for one week. Then come back to this page and take the self-test below.

· ·

SELF-TEST

1. Over the past week, was your diet well balanced with plenty of protein foods and not too much sugar?

YES   **NO**

· ·

Sleep and Rest

You would need adequate sleep and rest, even if you didn't have an anger problem. As a person with an anger problem, you need to pay close attention to how much sleep and rest you get. Inadequate sleep and rest will intensify your anger triggers by raising your inner tension level.

NOTE: If you have trouble sleeping on a regular basis, you may be suffering from insomnia. People who have insomnia usually have a long-standing problem with getting to sleep or staying asleep. As you recall from Chapter 5, insomnia is one of the symptoms of Post Traumatic Stress Disorder, or PTSD. Insomnia may also be a symptom of some other problem, whether emotional or physical. If you have a long-standing problem getting to sleep or staying asleep, and often get up in the morning feeling as though you haven't slept, then you should see a doctor. Your doctor may suggest a certain medication, or suggest that you go to a counselor in order to find out why you have a problem sleeping. You are strongly urged not to use non-prescribed drugs, including alcohol, to help yourself sleep. Drinking coffee or other caffeinated beverages before going to bed can also cause insomnia.

Try to establish regular bedtimes and regular wake-up times. Once you have established good sleep patterns you will feel more rested, and you will be less likely to get angry.

· ·

SELF-TEST

1. Do you get adequate sleep and rest?

YES   **NO**

2. When you get up in the morning, do you feel rested, or do you feel you need more sleep? Circle which is true for you.

Rested   Need more sleep

. . . .

Physical Exercise

Your body needs exercise. Regular exercise releases "feel good" chemicals from your brain. These "feel good" chemicals make you feel good about yourself. They have a positive effect on your self-esteem. Regular exercise also gives you a sense of accomplishment. Accomplishment is a valued feeling. You should exercise regularly, but you should not over-exercise.

There are many kinds of exercise. You could pump iron. You could walk or jog, swim or row a boat. You could climb stairs or do push-ups. The best kind of exercise programs involve movements that exercise all major muscle groups. An exercise program does not need to be excessively difficult; in fact it shouldn't be. Often it helps to have a workout partner. You could join a gym. You could go to karate classes. Having a workout partner or belonging to a gym or karate school could help you stay with an exercise program. Even though you may be young and feel in the best of health, you should have a physical check-up before beginning an exercise program.

. . . .

SELF-TEST

1. Name at least one kind of exercise you think you would enjoy.

. . . .

Relaxation

Relaxation is another important basic consideration. You need to know how to relax in order to deal effectively with stress. Stress is an unpleasant feeling, a negative feeling, a painful feeling. Stress increases your inner tension level. Therefore, stress is an anger trigger. In fact, for most, if not all, people stress is a major anger trigger. In the past you used anger and violence to reduce the heightened inner tension level created by stress. Now you need to learn how to deal with stress differently. One of the best ways to deal effectively with stress is by using a relaxation technique. The relaxation technique below will help you manage stress and reduce your tension level. It is an easy method. You can learn it quickly and you can benefit from it immediately.

A Relaxation Method to Help You Manage Stress

The Best Position to Use

The best position for relaxation is whatever works best for you. You need to find a comfortable position where you can sit for 10 to 20 minutes without cramping or falling asleep. You could sit cross-legged on the floor. You could sit in a chair. If you sit in a chair, sit up straight with your feet on the floor. That seems to works best for most people. Try different positions until you find one that works for you.

The Best Place to Relax

As with the best position, the best place is whatever works for you. It should be a private place where you can be alone in silence. If one place doesn't work, choose another place.

The Best Time to Relax

The best time to relax is whatever time of the day or night that suits you best. Of course you will want to choose a time that does not interfere with school, or with your part-time job if you have one.

How to Relax

You are encouraged to record on a CD or on your iPod or MP3 player, if you can, the relaxation steps outlined below. Then you can sit back and relax and listen to the instructions and not worry about leaving something out.

Relaxation is a learned process, a step-by-step procedure like riding a bicycle, driving a car, or brushing your teeth. Go to your place of relaxation and take the position you decided to use when you relax. Turn the lights down. Here are the steps:

1. Start by breathing slowly and deeply, and continue to breathe that way.

2. Relax your posture.

3. With your eyes open and continuing to breathe deeply and slowly, make three statements (silently, not aloud) about what you see. For example, "I see a chair over in the corner. I see shadows on the wall in the dim lamplight." Say the words on the out-breath.

At the end of the third statement, add, "And now I'm beginning to feel relaxed and calm." Now close your eyes and go to Step Four.

4. With your eyes closed and continuing to breathe deeply and slowly, make three statements about what you hear. Say the words on the out-breath, as before. For example, "I hear the sound of a dog barking in the distance. I hear the sound of water running in the kitchen. I hear the rhythmic sound of my own heartbeat, and now I'm beginning to feel more relaxed and calm."

Switching from what you see to what you hear allows your conscious mind to let go of visual images so that it can concentrate on what you hear.

5. Continuing the same breathing pattern, with your eyes shut, make three statements about what you are feeling, externally, saying the words as you breathe out. For example, "I can feel the pressure of my feet against the floor. I can feel the pressure of my back against the chair. I can feel the rise and fall of my chest as I breathe in and out, and now I feel calm and relaxed." This step allows your mind to let go of auditory input (what you hear) so that it can focus on what you are feeling.

By now you will have begun to relax. This method works by causing the mind to let go of the normal conscious state in a step-by-step fashion. One by one, your senses (sight, hearing, and touch) disengage. Your heart rate slows down. Your blood pressure decreases. Your body becomes relaxed. Your mind shifts its focus inside. Once you have relaxed your body, your mind will want to relax too. Think of some relaxing images and focus on them. If other kinds of images pop up in your mind and threaten to interrupt your relaxation, send them away and refocus on your relaxing images. With practice you will be able to relax quickly using this method. Practice this relaxation method at least once a day. Twice a day would be better.

If the relaxation technique above doesn't seem to work for you, you could take a relaxation training class. They are usually not expensive. In a relaxation class, you could learn a technique that might work better for you.

> **MESSAGE FROM GEORGE**
>
> *I'm George. I'm from Racine, Wisconsin. I'm fourteen years old, and I have a problem with anger. Sometimes I ate right, sometimes I didn't. Sometimes I went two or three weeks without a full night's sleep. I almost never exercised. When I did, I exercised too little or too much. I didn't know how to relax. Going without sleep, and not exercising, and my lousy eating habits, all had a bad effect on my mood. I got a book from my Health Class teacher and read up on nutrition. My gym teacher helped me get started on an exercise program. I stopped drinking coffee. My mood improved and I slept better. But I still felt stressed out—a lot. And I knew stress triggered my anger. So I learned the relaxation method described in this chapter. It was easy to learn. After a couple of weeks, I was able to relax more. Making these changes made it easier to deal with my anger.*
>
> *George*

Consult the phone directory Yellow Pages or the Internet to find out if there is an affordable relaxation class in your area.

. . . .

SELF-TEST

1. Circle the answer that best describes how you felt after doing the relaxation exercise above.

   (a) Very relaxed

   (b) A little relaxed

   (c) Not at all relaxed

NOTE: If you circled (b) or (c), don't give up. Usually, the more you use this or any other relaxation method, the better it will work for you. Practice the relaxation method for a week or so. If you don't get better results, then try a different method.

. . . .

Maintaining a Schedule

In order to maintain an effective anger recovery program, you will need to follow a schedule. You will need to schedule time for growth and development at each recovery level. You will need to schedule time for all of the basics. You will need to schedule meal times, so that you do not skip meals or eat poor meals on the run. You will need to schedule time for sleep and rest. You will need to schedule time for exercise, and time for relaxation. After you have referred to your daily schedule and followed it for a period of time, it will become a part of your daily life. Then you will not need to refer to it as often. Using your written schedule, you will teach yourself the self-discipline that you will need in order to be your very best.

Here is an example of a personal schedule that covers the basic considerations:

DAILY SCHEDULE					
Breakfast	**Lunch**	**Dinner**	**Exercise**	**Relaxation**	**Sleep**
Time: 7:00 AM	12:30 PM	6:00 PM	7:00 PM	10:00 PM	11:00 PM
Daily	**Daily**	**Daily**	**M, W, F**	**Daily**	**Daily**

Of course, when you make your schedule you need to consider your family and their schedule, and adjust your schedule to match up with theirs. Also, you will need to factor in your school schedule. And if you have a part-time job, you will, of course, need to take your work schedule into account too. Your personal schedule must not interfere with your family and school and work obligations.

· ·

SELF-TEST

1. Make a daily schedule that covers all four basic considerations. Use the form provided below.

   NOTE: Build a little flexibility into your schedule. Cut yourself some slack. There will be times when you can't stick to your schedule. But do your best.

DAILY SCHEDULE

	Breakfast	Lunch	Dinner	Exercise	Relaxation	Sleep
Time:	_____	_____	_____	_____	_____	_____
	Daily	Daily	Daily	M, W, F	Daily	Daily

· ·

CHAPTER TWELVE

Intercept and Stop Anger Triggers

What you think about most of the time causes how you feel most of the time. If you think positive thoughts most of the time, you will feel good most of the time. If you think negative thoughts most of the time, you will feel bad most of the time. Thinking negative thoughts keeps you stuck in the anger process (in the river), because negative thoughts lead to bad feelings, and bad feelings are anger triggers.

In this chapter you will learn some ways to deal with negative thoughts that lead to the feelings that trigger your angry behavior. You will learn how to think positive thoughts that make you feel self-empowered.

Maintain a Positive Mental Focus

What you focus on, mentally, is what you are thinking about at any given time. You look at certain mental images in your mind, you listen to certain mental sounds. That is what thinking means. In a way, it is like watching DVDs and listening to CDs. You think in mental images and mental sounds. Most of the time you are not aware of what you are thinking about, but you need to learn to be aware of what you think about. What kind of DVDs do you watch inside your mind most of the time? What kind of mental CDs do you listen to?

Angry people focus on negative thoughts most of the time. That is, you watch, inside your mind, DVDs that you associate with anger and violence. You probably focus on mental images that show how someone hurt you in the past. Also, you probably listen to old mental CDs that you associate with anger. You probably listen to old CDs of what someone said that hurt you. Thinking about these images and recordings consistently means that you maintain a negative mental focus.

As you have already learned, a metaphor is a comparison. You learned to think of anger as being like the Niagara Falls and Niagara River. When you say something is like something else, you are using a metaphor.

Here is another useful metaphor. It will help you understand how your brain works. Your memories are like DVDs and CDs. Memories stored on DVDs are movies. The movies are often in full color and with surround sound. The CDs are like sound bites. Sound bites are fragments of dialogue or music. The movies and sound bites are stored in the part of your brain called memory. Your memory is like a gigantic media storage cabinet. Everything you have ever seen or heard was recorded on a DVD or CD, and is now stored in your media cabinet—everything. All of your experiences, good or bad, happy or sad, have been recorded and stored. Your brain, which is like a recording and playback machine, can replay any of these stored memories. All you have to do is think of which recorded memory you want to watch or which to listen to. Your brain then plays it back for you to watch or listen to. Very often, you don't have to think

MESSAGE FROM SEAN

Hi. I didn't know how much time I spent thinking negative thoughts. The kind of thoughts that made me have negative feelings that triggered my anger. When I started paying attention, I found out I was thinking negative thoughts most of the time! No wonder I was angry so much. I used to think about what people had said or done in the past to hurt me. It was just like watching old DVDs and listening to old CDs. Then I'd think about what I'd do, or like to do, to pay them back. I made my own DVDs using my imagination. I'm a writer, so I was pretty good at it. Using my imagination, I made images in my mind of the people I wanted to get back at. Big, bright clear pictures. I used my imagination to make DVDs of what I'd do to get my revenge—in full color with surround sound. Yes! I listened to old CDs, too. I could remember every word someone said, even if it was five years ago. Especially if the words had hurt me. But most of the time I wasn't even aware when I was focusing on all that negative stuff. The DVDs and CDs played out just below my awareness. Sometimes I was aware of my negative mental focus. At those times, I can remember purposely holding on to those pictures and sounds. Those old DVDs and CDs that I watched and listened to made me have negative feelings. And the negative feelings triggered my anger. The revenge DVDs I made with my imagination made me feel powerful. And they made me want to go and do what I was thinking about. It was like I was rehearsing for a school play. But when I went and did what I was rehearsing, believe me it wasn't play. Neither were the consequences. They were real. Yeah, I found out I focused on negative thoughts at least 50% of the time. Now I know how to change that. Now I can press Stop, replace the DVD or CD causing the negative feelings with a DVD or CD that'll give me positive feelings, and press Start. Now, that's how I stop myself from doing something dumb.

Sean

of a certain memory in order to make it play back. A certain thing can happen in your outer environment, or someone can say something, and all of a sudden an old movie or an old sound recording starts to play. You find yourself for no apparent reason recalling an event that happened yesterday, or last week, or 10 years ago. The old movie or sound bite starts to play on its own.

Every DVD and every CD stored in your mental media cabinet contains recorded images and sounds. The images and sounds always cause you to have certain kinds of feelings. Depending on the kinds of images and sounds, you will have either positive feelings or negative feelings. Sometimes the images and sounds you watch and listen to are not as crisp and clear as they once were. But sometimes the images and sounds—even some that are very old—are of such high quality, it is as though the memory is brand-new. The DVDs and CDs upon which traumatic memories are stored seem never to wear out. The quality of the images and sounds doesn't seem to fade with time. The DVD or CD doesn't skip or become garbled. The images and sounds recorded on the old discs are almost too good—too good ever to be forgotten.

The DVDs and CDs that are stored in your media cabinet also act as cues. Cues signal your body to produce feelings that your brain associates with the recorded images and sounds. These mental images and sounds acting as cues cause the feelings that trigger your anger.

In order to change your angry behavior, you need to change your mental focus. In other words, you need to change what you think about most of the time. You can learn how to change your mental focus. You can learn how to take control of which DVDs and which CDs you watch and listen to. In order to change your mental focus, you need to notice when you are watching old movies or listening to old sounds that cause you to have negative feelings. Because, as you have already learned, negative feelings are anger triggers.

Once you learn to notice when you are watching movies or listening to sound bites that cause you to have negative feelings, then you can change your mental focus. You can push Stop on your playback machine and remove the DVD or CD which is causing you to have negative feelings. Then you can reach into your media cabinet and select a different movie or sound bite disc. You can select one that gives you positive feelings, and then push Start.

Using the metaphor which compares memories to DVDs and CDs, you can learn skills that will help you change what you think about most of the time. And changing what you think about most of the time will change how you feel most of the time. You will feel less angry, and more relaxed and calm. You will feel more confident and assertive. The skills which follow will help you change your mental focus.

SELF-TEST

1. What you think about causes how you feel.

   TRUE   FALSE

2. Thinking negative thoughts keeps you stuck in the anger process (in the Niagara River), because negative thoughts lead to bad feelings, and bad feelings are anger triggers.

   TRUE   FALSE

3. You look at certain mental images in your mind, and you listen to certain mental sounds. That is what thinking means.

   TRUE   FALSE

4. In a way, thinking is like watching DVDs and listening to CDs.

   TRUE   FALSE

5. As a person with an anger problem, you probably often watch mental movies and listen to mental sound bites that you associate with anger and violence.

   TRUE   FALSE

6. In his message on page 130, Sean said he used to use his imagination to make his own revenge DVDs. Have you ever used your imagination to make revenge DVDs?

   YES   NO

. . . .

The Skills

Skill #1: Look at a Special Photo or Picture

You now know about the importance of mental focus. You know focusing consistently on mental images that you associate with anger keeps you stuck in the anger habit. Now you will learn how to change your mental focus.

A. Read all the instructions before you actually use the skill.

Do you have a special photo you carry with you in your wallet or purse, or on your iPod or cell phone that makes you feel good when you look at it? Maybe you have a photo of your girl friend or boy friend, or of your dog or cat. Maybe you have a picture from nature that makes you feel good. If you do not have a special photo or picture, you should obtain one. Then when a trigger occurs, look at the photo or picture that makes you feel good. As you look at it, relax your posture and slow down your breathing. You will automatically start feeling whatever good feelings you associate with the special photo or picture. If you associate a good feeling with the person or thing in the special photo or picture, then you will automatically feel good.

Holding the special photo or picture in your hand, now close your eyes and think of something in the past that triggered your anger. Thinking about it will make you feel some of the anger again. When you begin to feel some of that anger, open your eyes and look at your special photo or picture. While looking at the photo or picture, relax your posture and slow down your breathing.

Now check on how you feel. On a scale from 1 to 10, what was your level of anger before looking at the special photo or picture? The higher the number, the higher your anger level. Circle the number that best describes how you felt.

$$1 \quad 2 \quad 3 \quad 4 \quad 5 \quad 6 \quad 7 \quad 8 \quad 9 \quad 10$$

Now circle the number that best describes your anger level after using the skill.

$$1 \quad 2 \quad 3 \quad 4 \quad 5 \quad 6 \quad 7 \quad 8 \quad 9 \quad 10$$

If your anger level was still more than a 2 or 3, try the skill again. Or select a different photo or picture, and then try the skill again.

Skill #2: Watch a Calming or Relaxing Mental DVD

A. Read all the instructions before you actually use the skill.

First close your eyes and think of a time in the past when you were angry. You can use the same one you used for Skill #1 if you want. How angry do you now feel, as you recall that time in the past when you were angry? Circle the correct number on the scale below.

$$1 \quad 2 \quad 3 \quad 4 \quad 5 \quad 6 \quad 7 \quad 8 \quad 9 \quad 10$$

Now close your eyes and think of a scene from a DVD or a CD sound bite that always causes you to feel calm or relaxed. There are plenty to choose from in your mental media cabinet. Search until you find one. When you find that calming or relaxing disc, press Play. Let the new disc play for a minute or two. Now check how you feel. Now circle the number that best describes your anger level.

1 2 3 4 5 6 7 8 9 10

If your anger level is still more than a 2 or 3, try the skill again. Or think of a different movie or sound bite that made you feel calm or relaxed, and then try the skill again.

This is one of the most useful skills you will learn from this book. Use your imagination and creativity to find other ways to use this skill.

Skill #3: Listen to Relaxing Music

Listening to relaxing music changes how you feel. Shakespeare said it "soothes the wild beast." Some people compare their anger habit to a wild beast. Does it sometimes feel that way to you? You may find relaxing music to be a good way to quiet the wild beast inside you. Listening to relaxing music will help you maintain a positive mental focus. Listening to "gangster rap" will have the opposite effect. It will wake up the wild beast.

Find a CD that helps you relax. Then follow the instructions below.

A. Sit next to a CD player. Put your relaxing CD in the player. Don't play the CD just yet.

B. Now think of something that made you angry in the past. Notice the level of your anger using a scale from 1 to 10.

C. When you begin to feel some anger, push Play on the CD player and listen to the relaxing music. Listen to the music for 5-10 minutes.

Circle the number that best describes your anger level after listening to the relaxing CD for 5-10 minutes.

1   2   3   4   5   6   7   8   9   10

Skill #4: Watch a Humorous DVD to Interrupt Triggers

Humor is a powerful way to interrupt anger triggers, a good way to get out of the river. Humor is a good anchor. Even when you are close to the Falls, sometimes humor can get you out in time.

A famous sports hero suffered a severe injury that caused him a lot of pain. He didn't want to use too much pain medication. He believed it would have a negative effect on his recovery. He felt powerless over the pain. Feeling powerless triggered his anger. Aware of the power of humor, he borrowed comedy DVDs from his friends. The sports hero discovered that watching a humorous DVD for two hours provided him with two hours of pain-free time. Watching the humorous DVD also relieved his anger!

A.   Read all the instructions before you use Skill #4.

First, buy a DVD movie that makes you laugh, or borrow one from a friend. Put it in your DVD player, or in your laptop or PC. If you don't have a DVD player at home, ask permission to use one of the school laptops or PCs. Don't push Play just yet.

Now think of a memory of a time in the past when you were angry. Once you have found that angry memory, let it play out in your mind for a minute or two. Circle the level of your anger.

1   2   3   4   5   6   7   8   9   10

Now press Play and start the humorous movie. Watch five minutes of the DVD, then press Pause and check your anger level.

1   2   3   4   5   6   7   8   9   10

If your anger level is still a 3 or higher, press Play and watch the humorous movie for five more minutes. Then check your anger level again.

1   2   3   4   5   6   7   8   9   10

By now, your anger level is probably down to a 3 or even lower. But if your anger level is still above 3, continue watching the movie to the end and then check your level. What was your level of anger after watching the entire movie?

1   2   3   4   5   6   7   8   9   10

Skill #5: Listen to a Humorous CD to Interrupt Anger Triggers

Listening to a humorous CD will interrupt your anger process in the same way as watching a humorous DVD. Buy, or borrow from a friend, a humorous CD. Put the CD in your player, but do not as yet press Play. As in Skill #4, choose a memory of a time in the past when you were angry. Make it a different memory from the one you used in Skill #4. When your anger level reaches about 5, press Play and listen to the humorous CD. Spend about 10 minutes listening to it.

After listening to the humorous CD for 10 minutes, press Stop and circle your anger level using the scale of 1 to 10.

1   2   3   4   5   6   7   8   9   10

If your anger level is still more than 3, press Play again and listen to the CD for 10 more minutes, and then check your anger level.

1   2   3   4   5   6   7   8   9   10

If your anger level is still more than 3, continue to listen to the humorous CD until your anger level is no more than a 2 on the scale.

Skill #6: Use Physical Exercise to Interrupt Anger Triggers

So far, you have learned five skills to interrupt anger triggers. The first five skills you learned involved the application of mental skills. Now here is a skill that applies physical exercise to the problem of anger management.

Physical exercise is another good way to interrupt anger triggers. It is another effective anchor. There are many types of exercise to chose from. Choose one that you can do easily without a lot of equipment. Choose a form of exercise you feel you will be most likely to use, and which you can easily do in your house, in your room, or outdoors.

Exercise usually puts a person in a positive mood. When you are in a positive mood, you often think positive thoughts automatically. Therefore, exercise is another good way to help you maintain a positive mental focus.

There are many forms of exercise that you could use to interrupt anger triggers. Some examples are listed below.

- Pump iron
- Do push-ups
- Tai Chi
- Yoga
- Walk or run
- Do deep knee bends
- Dance
- Gymnastics

Some of the types of exercise listed above may appeal to you, or none of them may appeal to you. If the exercises listed above do not appeal to you, then think of a type of exercise that you would like to do. Just make sure the type of exercise you choose is one that you can do at home or outdoors. When you think of a type of exercise that you would like to use as a skill to interrupt anger triggers, follow the instructions below.

A. **Read all the instructions before you actually do Skill #6.**

Think of a time in the past when you were angry. If you want, you can use the same memory you used in Skill #1. Write down your anger level using the scale 1-10.

Now start doing the type of exercise you chose to use in order to interrupt your anger. Exercise vigorously for five minutes and check your anger level again. If it is still more than a 2, exercise for another five minutes. If after five more minutes your anger level is still more than a 2, sit down in a comfortable chair. Then use one of the mental skills you used earlier. Doing so will enhance the effects of the physical skill you just completed.

Skill # 7: Make a Gratitude List

It is easy to forget the good things you have in your life, especially in times of stress, because when you feel stressed, your mental focus becomes negative.

Maintaining awareness of the good things in your life creates a positive mental focus. It makes you feel grateful. If you are mentally aware of some of the good things in your life, you will be less likely to get angry when a trigger happens. But you need a way to be aware of the good things in your life. Making a gratitude list that you can look at will help you stay mentally aware of the good things. You can look at your gratitude list and see what you have to be grateful for. It will allow you to make a useful comparison. You can compare the things on your gratitude list to whatever is triggering your anger, and that will help you keep things in perspective. It will help you see what is really important in your life and what is not.

A gratitude list will help you maintain a positive mental focus. Below is a list of things that anyone could be grateful for.

> **MESSAGE FROM BRIAN AND ERIK**
>
> *We're Brian and Erik, two teenage brothers with an anger problem. We were born with Muscular Dystrophy (MD). The disease has really done a number on us. We both have to be fed through a tube inserted through the stomach wall. We have trouble walking, breathing, sitting, standing. Maybe we'll live to be forty, maybe not. MD keeps getting worse, never better. So what are we grateful for? We're both grateful for our family and our friends. I (Brian) am also grateful for my faith. My brother Erik is also grateful for when he could play sports, before the disease took over. Hey, don't pity us. Be inspired.*
>
> *Brian* & **Erik**

- Being alive
- Having food to eat
- Being able to talk
- Having eyes and ears
- Being able to breathe

Chances are you have all of the things on the list, above, in your life. But there must be many other things you have that you are grateful for, too.

Make a list of things you are grateful for and make a copy of the list. Keep the copy with you. Each time you feel triggered into the anger process, read your gratitude list.

I am grateful for...

_____

_____

_____

_____

_____

_____

_____

_____

_____

Skill #8: Using Self-Commands to Interrupt Triggers

You can use brief self-commands to interrupt your anger triggers. A self-command is a word or short phrase that helps you quickly change negative feelings into positive feelings. Self-commands make good anchors to throw on shore and pull yourself out of the river.

Some examples of self-commands you can use to interrupt anger triggers are listed below.

- Change your breathing!
- Anger is pain!
- Violence is never justified!
- Stop!

When you use one of your self-commands, put energy into it. You don't have to yell, but you should use a strong, assertive voice. You can say the command silently, if circumstances make it inappropriate to say it out loud. If you utter the self-command silently, you can still say it with feeling. Inside your mind, it should sound like a loud thought.

Copy the self-commands listed. Write them on paper small enough to fit in your wallet. Then follow the instructions below.

1. Look at your list of self-commands.

2. Choose a word or phrase from the list to use as a tool to interrupt your anger.

3. Now think of something that made you angry in the past. In your mind, notice the level of your anger on a scale from 1 to 10. When you feel some of the anger, look at the self-command you chose.

4. Using a strong voice, say the self-command. Say it with feeling. What was your anger level on a scale from 1 to 10 after using the self-command? You could also record your self-commands on your MP3 player or on your iPod. Try raising the volume to the loud position when you play back your self-commands, and see what happens.

In this chapter, you have learned eight skills to help yourself maintain a positive mental focus. The skills you learned will help you to interrupt anger triggers. The skills represent choices.

> **MESSAGE FROM TOMMY**
>
> *My name is Tommy. I'm from Washington, D.C. I'm almost sixteen. I knew I had an anger habit, and I knew I wanted to recover. I'd start my day in a positive frame of mind. Like I knew I should. I'd say to myself, "Today I'm not going to be stupid. I'm not going to go over the Falls." Then some little thing would happen, or maybe a lot of little things would happen in a row. And before I knew it, wham! Over the Falls. I needed skills. I needed a lot of anchors. I learned some of the skills in this chapter. Then things got better. Finally, I had things to do that would work. With my new skills, I could get out of the river before it was too late. Then I learned some more skills and added them to the ones I already knew. My box of anger management tools got bigger and I felt more able to manage my behavior. Later, things got even better. The more skills I learned, the better things got. I'm still learning new ways to manage my anger. I plan to keep learning.*
>
> *Tommy*

• •

SELF-TEST

1. List 3-5 other self-commands you could use to interrupt your anger triggers, and practice using them.

_____

_____

_____

_____

_____

• •

CHAPTER THIRTEEN

Avoid Anger Triggers

It is important to know how to interrupt triggers and get out of the anger process. It is also important to know what to avoid, so that you will be less likely to end up in the anger process in the first place.

Avoid Alcohol and Other Drugs

Alcohol or other drug use is involved in more than 50% of cases of family violence and in more than 50% of assaults and murders. Alcohol and other drugs such as meth, crack cocaine, steroids, and some tranquilizers intensify the feelings that trigger anger. If you really want to stop using anger and violence, you should not use alcohol. And you should not use other drugs which have not been prescribed by a doctor. You must be careful even when using prescribed drugs.

Warning: If you presently need to use medication prescribed by a doctor, do not stop taking the medication without checking with your doctor. Use your medication only as prescribed. Read the warnings on the labels. If the medication seems to make your anger worse, bring it to the attention of your doctor.

Combinations of certain drugs are even more dangerous. For example, the use of alcohol combined with meth or cocaine or sleeping pills. Combining these substances can have deadly results. You cannot afford to use any substance or combinations of any substances that will make your anger worse.

Alcohol definitely makes anger worse. Just a couple of drinks interferes with your judgment. That makes you more likely to say and do angry things. Use of other drugs, such as meth or cocaine, both of which are types of "speed," have the same effect. They impair thinking and make anger worse. When you use alcohol or other drugs, you are less likely to use your anger management skills.

Some people who have an anger problem use alcohol and other drugs in order to intensify their anger. Here is a case which illustrates the deadly effects of mixing alcohol with other drugs. A young man got drunk in Chicago on a mixture of alcohol and drugs. He went into a rage and murdered six young female nursing students. He did not even remember doing it. He had never been violent before. He died in prison.

You are strongly urged to stop using all mood-altering drugs unless prescribed by a physician, including marijuana. If you associate marijuana with peaceful feelings, you are making a big mistake. Marijuana users who have a problem with anger may become violent. The risk is highest when your supply of the drug runs out, or when you are in situations where you cannot use the drug. At those times your baseline tension level climbs above normal. Feelings of fear, anxiety, frustration, and other negative emotions that may trigger anger can become much more intense when the level of marijuana in your blood decreases.

If you have a problem with alcohol or other drugs, seek help now.

. . . .

SELF-TEST

1. The man who killed the student nurses was under the influence of alcohol and drugs.

    TRUE   FALSE

2. The man who killed the nurses didn't remember what he had done.

    TRUE   FALSE

3. Were you ever violent when drinking or when using other drugs?

    YES   NO

4. You have an anger problem. If you drink, or use other drugs not prescribed by a doctor, why should you stop?

. . . .

Avoid Places Where Heavy Drinking or Drug Use Takes Place

Most violence ending in injury or death takes place where there is heavy drinking or drug use. You may not use alcohol or other drugs, but you would still be at high risk for acting out angry feelings if you hang out or go to parties where alcohol and other drugs are used. Those at the party who are under the influence may say or do something which could cause you to have a feeling that triggers your anger.

SELF-TEST

1. Have you ever been violent in a place where there was heavy alcohol or drug use, even if you weren't drinking or using a drug?

YES   NO

Avoid the Use of Anabolic Steroids (Growth Drugs)

Some professional athletes have been using steroids (growth drugs) since the 1960s. Steroids increase body strength and muscle mass, no doubt about it. Weightlifters and bodybuilders were the first to use steroids. The use of steroids has become more widespread in recent years. Among teenagers, steroid use is still increasing at an alarming rate.

There is no doubt that steroids improve athletic performance. But the use of steroids has some very bad side effects. Even in young people, steroids can cause serious health problems such as strokes and heart attacks. They can even cause cancer.

Steroid use has another serious side effect. Steroids are strongly linked to increased aggression and violent behavior. People who use steroids are much more likely to be violent. This is true even for people who don't otherwise have a problem with anger. Steroid users call it "roid rage." Steroid use by people ,who have an anger habit is especially dangerous. Combining steroids with alcohol or other drugs such as meth or cocaine can even

> **MESSAGE FROM TERRY**
>
> *My name is Terry. I've got a real anger problem. But I'm doing better now, a lot better. My anger problem started at thirteen, when I started lifting weights. I'm fifteen now. Somebody I met at the gym turned me on to steroids, and I got strong real fast. The 'roids made me feel more confident, but I noticed they made my anger worse too. After I got on steroids, I started having trouble at school because of my anger. I got into a fight with a kid during gym class one day. I went completely out of control, in a fit of "roid rage." I beat the kid up so bad, they had me arrested. I got sent to a detention center. I got expelled for a whole semester and got put on probation for two years. I felt ashamed and stupid. If you have a problem with anger, don't use steroids, man, just don't.*
>
> *Terry*

cause a person to have a brief psychotic episode. A brief psychotic episode is a form of temporary insanity. People who become temporarily insane as a result of combing steroids with alcohol or other drugs sometimes become violently angry and may harm others or themselves. In such cases, the anger is often not a result of a negative feeling such as fear or embarrassment. In such cases the combination of the drugs acting on the brain chemistry is often the anger trigger.

· ·

SELF-TEST

1. Even in young people, steroid use can cause serious health problems.

TRUE   **FALSE**

2. Combining steroid drugs with alcohol or other drugs can cause a person to become temporarily insane.

TRUE   **FALSE**

· ·

Whenever Possible, Avoid Other People Who Have Problems With Anger and Rage

Whenever possible, you are strongly urged to stop associating with other angry people. Especially if they are not willing to change their behavior. Continuing to associate with people who are unwilling to do something about their anger very likely will keep you stuck in your old anger pattern.

One of your family members may have an anger problem. Of course you will be unable to avoid a family member who has an anger problem. There may be a few other people you cannot avoid who may have an anger problem. In these instances, you can only work your recovery program all the harder. But whenever possible, avoid people who are still stuck in anger and rage.

· ·

SELF-TEST

1. Are some people you associate with stuck in anger and rage?

YES   **NO**

2. Are you willing to change whom you associate with whenever necessary and whenever possible?

YES   NO

. . . .

Avoid Media Violence

The mass media (TV, radio, newspapers, magazines, the Internet) shapes behavior. To a very great extent, the mass media determines how we behave. The media often presents to your eyes and ears role models who use violence to get what they want. The media also presents images of violence over and over again. The mass media helps create the violence that threatens to tear society apart. It sometimes seems to make heroes out of killers. If nothing else, the mass media gives violent people a lot of attention. Watching violent movies and television shows will increase your anger. Reading books or newspaper articles with violent themes will have the same result. Popular songs that glamorize violence will also make your problem worse.

Participating in violent video games will increase your aggression. Video games with violent themes are very popular. Studies have shown that this type of entertainment increases violent behavior across all age ranges, and all ethnic groups. You are strongly urged, therefore, to strictly limit the time you spend playing video games with a primarily violent theme. Or, better yet, stop playing them altogether.

You are strongly urged to reduce your exposure to media violence. Carefully select what you watch, what you read, what you listen to, and what kinds of games you play. You are a person with an anger problem. You cannot afford to expose yourself to media programming that will only make your problem worse.

MESSAGE FROM SEAN

I didn't watch much television, but I sure was hooked on games. Especially the ones that had a lot of violence. They were exciting to play. I used to spend four or five hours a week playing games. So for four or five hours a week, I was exposed to a lot of violent action. I knew it wasn't real, but my brain and body didn't seem to know that. If I felt a little down on myself, or I was just feeling kinda blah, and I played one of the games that was full of a lot of violence, pretty soon I'd start to feel different. I'd end up feeling excited and, like, powerful. I got a high from it. I was still playing those same kind of games after I decided to do something about my anger problem. That's when I noticed that the games were having a bad effect. They definitely increased my tension level, and they definitely made my aggressive feelings worse. If I was already angry, playing the violent games made my anger worse. At times playing one of those games made me want to go and act out my anger. I thought playing violent video games would have the opposite effect. I thought it would help me reduce my inner tension. But it didn't. Usually, it made it worse. It made my tension level go higher, not lower. I don't play violent games anymore. I can't risk it.

Sean

SELF-TEST

1 Think of the last time you watched a violent TV program or movie. As you watched the program, did you notice an increase in baseline tension in your body?

YES   NO

2. In a few words, explain why Sean decided not to play violent DVD games anymore.

• •

Avoid Venting

Venting is a special form of anger. Venting is yelling, or beating a pillow with your fists, or stomping your feet. Venting is physically aggressive actions or words. But the aggressive actions or words used when you vent your anger are usually not directed at people or their property, or at animals.

Venting was once thought to drain off the tension produced by anger. But you are a person with an anger habit. Very likely, the kind of venting described here is a part of your anger pattern. As a person who has a problem with anger, venting is like practicing your anger. It reinforces your anger problem. Therefore, venting will only help keep you stuck in the anger process. It will only keep you stuck in the Niagara River. People who do not use anger like a drug may safely vent once in a while. But as a person with a serious anger problem, you cannot safely vent. You need to learn other ways to deal with frustration and other anger triggers.

> ### MESSAGE FROM SAM
>
> *My name is Sam. I was born and raised in the Bronx. I'm seventeen. I did my anger right up front. I was loud. I hit things, I threw things. When I first decided to stop my violent behavior, I used venting as a way to deal with my anger triggers. I pounded pillows. I broke useless things against the basement wall. I went to the gym and punched and kicked the heavy bag. Venting left me feeling drained and tired, but it didn't help me change my angry behavior. Venting made it worse. It reinforced my anger habit. I found other ways to deal with anger triggers. I had to.*
>
> *Sam*

Road Rage

If you are over sixteen, you may now have a driver's license. If you have a license and drive a car, do you use anger and rage while driving? If you do, your angry behavior while driving a car is called "road rage." Even if you do not use your car as a weapon, as some people do, when you are behaving in an angry way behind the wheel of a car you are putting others and yourself at risk for serious injury or even death.

Shaking your fist and yelling and making angry gestures while driving are examples of road rage behavior. When you are shaking your fist and yelling and making angry gestures, your driving skills become impaired. In fact, driving a car while angry is like driving under the influence of alcohol or some other drug. Angry behavior while driving a car may cause you to make decisions that are not safe. When you are angry, you may drive too fast. Your anger may cause you to take chances that you would otherwise not take. People who are angry while driving cause accidents which injure and kill many people every year.

. . . .

SELF-TEST

1. Venting is aggressive actions or words which are usually not aimed at people or their property, or at animals.

TRUE   FALSE

2. As a person with an anger problem, you need to learn other ways to deal with anger triggers.

TRUE   FALSE

4. Using the form of anger called road rage is like driving under the influence of alcohol or other drugs.

TRUE   FALSE

5. Instead of venting, you could use the skills you are learning. List three skills you could use instead of venting.

    1. _____

    2. _____

    3. _____

. . . .

Anger and Weapons

More than 50% of murders are committed by angry people who own guns. You may have access to, or even possess, guns or other weapons. You may own knives or other potentially deadly weapons.

If you own weapons of any kind, you are strongly urged to appropriately dispose of all your weapons now.

· ·

SELF-TEST

1. Why should anyone who has an anger problem dispose of their weapons now? Explain in a few words.

· ·

CHAPTER FOURTEEN

Special Methods and Skills
for Controlling Anger

In Chapter 12 you were asked to think of your memories as being stored on mental DVDs and CDs. Memories stored on DVDs are like full-color movies with surround sound. Memories stored on CDs are like sound bites. You learned that the DVDs and CDs are stored in the part of your brain called memory, which is like a huge media storage cabinet. Everything you have ever seen or heard was recorded on a DVD or CD, and is now stored in your media cabinet. All of your experiences have been recorded and stored. In Chapter 12, you also learned that your brain is like a DVD recorder and playback machine, and can replay any of your stored memories. To use Special Skill #1, described later in this chapter, you are going to pay special attention to the idea that the brain is like a DVD recorder and player. You are going to use the DVD player remote pad device to help yourself deal effectively with stubborn memory cues. As you learned in Chapter 12, the DVDs and CDs that are stored in your media cabinet also act as cues. You learned that cues signal your body to produce feelings that your brain associates with the recorded images, and that these mental images cause the feelings that trigger your anger.

In order to change your angry behavior, you need to change your mental focus. In other words, you need to change what you think about most of the time. You can learn how to change your mental focus. You can learn how to take control of which DVDs and which CDs you watch and listen to. In order to change your mental focus, you need to notice when you are watching old movies or listening to old sounds that cause you to have negative feelings. Because, as you have already learned, negative feelings are anger triggers.

Once you learn to notice when you are watching movies or listening to sound bites that cause you to have negative feelings, then you can change your mental focus. You can push Stop on your playback machine and remove the DVD or CD which is causing you to have negative feelings. Then you can reach into your media cabinet and select a different movie or sound bite disc. You can select one that gives you positive feelings, and then push Start.

Anger Cues

Review: What Are Cues?

As you have already learned, a cue is something you see or hear. An anger cue is something you see or hear that leads to an anger trigger.

Memory Cues

Some cues are memories of things you have seen or heard. They are memory cues. A cue is a signal to do something. An orchestra conductor "cues" each musician with a signal that tells each musician when to start playing or to stop playing. A red light at a corner is a cue to stop. The sound of an ambulance siren is a cue to pull over to the curb. The smell of food cooking is a cue that tells your mouth to start producing saliva. An anger cue signals your body and brain to produce an anger trigger. It tells your body and brain to produce a bad feeling.

Memories of things that happened to you also act as cues, and can be as strong or stronger than cues that happen in the present. Remembering something you saw or heard "cues" you to have the same feelings you had when it originally happened. Memories of bad things make you have bad feelings again. Memories of good things make you have good feelings again.

Memories of things that cause you to have negative feelings, such as fear or frustration, act as anger triggers. Chances are you have many such memories. Memories that cause you emotional pain when they pop into your mind; memories that act as anger cues. Memories that act as anger cues cause your tension level to rise. Recalling these memories keeps you stuck in the anger process. Some of the memories which are cues for the feelings that trigger anger are very stubborn. They pop into your conscious mind often, and it is hard to keep from focusing on them. But you can learn how to deal with memory cues that, in the past, kept you stuck in anger and rage. You can learn how to let go of them, so that they no longer cause you to have feelings that trigger your anger.

Scenario One

Suppose someone said something to you in the past that caused you to feel embarrassed, and the feeling of embarrassment triggered your anger and sent you plunging into the Niagara River. Suppose you are walking down the street a few days later and happen to see that same person again. How do you suppose you would react? Do you think you would get angry all over again? Chances are you would. The person who said something that caused you to feel embarrassed in the past now would be an anger cue in the present. The person's face would act as a cue, causing you to recall what was said or done that produced the feeling of embarrassment. You would experience the feeling of embarrassment again, and the feeling of embarrassment would trigger your anger all over again. The person's face would act as an anger cue until you did something to change the cue.

Scenario Two

Suppose someone said something that caused you embarrassment, but you never saw the person again. Suppose you are walking down the street a few days later. You don't actually see the person on the street, but a memory of his face pops suddenly into your mind. Inside your mind, the memory looks big and bright. You might even remember small details, perhaps the small tattoo on his hand. Would the memory of the person who embarrassed you cause you to feel angry again? It would! Because acting as a cue, the memory would cause you to re-experience the feeling of embarrassment that triggered your anger at the time of the actual event. In other words, the memory would act as a cue. It would act as a memory cue. And the feeling of embarrassment would act as an anger trigger. You would become angry all over again. The good news is that you can learn how to deal with stubborn memory cues.

Dealing With Stubborn Memory Cues

As you learned in Chapter 12, there are different kinds of memories. There are visual memories (things you remember seeing) and auditory memories (things you remember hearing). Visual memories are made up of certain qualities, such as brightness and size.

When you recall a visual memory, you see it like a photograph or a DVD image projected on a screen inside your mind. The quality of the brightness of the image attached to a particular memory is a very important quality when it comes to recalling the memory. The brightness of the image that makes up a visual memory ranges from very bright to very dim.

All visual memories produce feelings, when you think of the memories. Some visual memories cause strong feelings; some visual memories cause weak feelings. Whether the feeling you experience because of recalling a particular memory is strong or weak depends entirely on how bright or dim the image of the memory looks to you when you see it on the screen inside your mind. Bright memories cause strong feelings; very bright memories cause very strong feelings. Dim memories cause weak feelings; very dim memories cause very weak feelings.

Most visual memories fade out and become dim and uninteresting with the passing of time, but not always. Sometimes memories remain very bright for a very long time, especially if they are the result of powerful events that made you feel very strong feelings in the first place. Old faded memories won't give you trouble. There is not enough brightness left to interest your brain. The faded-out memories slip down out of sight, down into the murky bottom layers of the mind. These old, faded-out memories almost never pop back up to the surface.

Memory cues that remain very bright are the ones that will give you trouble, especially the ones you associate with strong negative feelings such as fear. Their brightness makes them lighter; they float closer to the surface of your mind. Even bright memories won't give you trouble all of the time, but they are always lurking just below the surface. They knife through your conscious mind like sharks cutting the surface of the water showing only their dorsal fin.

Trying to force down a big bright memory won't work. It is like forcing a beach ball down under the water. What happens when you let go? The beach ball pops back to the surface. Right? In fact, it often pops completely out of the water! That's what happens when you force down a big bright memory; it pops back up as soon as you let go, and for a while it looks even bigger and brighter.

Here's how to deal with a stubborn memory cue: learn how to reduce the brightness of the image representing the memory. Special Skill #1 will help you reduce the brightness from any stubborn memory cue that keeps you stuck in the anger process. The skill changes the memory cue. It extinguishes the cue. It puts out the memory cue's light. Then the memory sinks below the surface, way down deep where it belongs, and it stays there. Practice this skill with all of your stubborn memory cues. It is another way to change your mental focus in order to change how you feel.

Before proceeding with Special Skill #1, you will first need to make a list of some of your stubborn memory cues, ones that create feelings that trigger your anger. List the ones that are the most stubborn. They will be the biggest and brightest. Two or three stubborn memories will be plenty to start with. An example of a stubborn memory cue might be one of the following:

- A memory of someone who beat you up when you were a kid. When you think of the person, you feel strong feelings of fear and anxiety, then you get angry.

- A memory of someone who did something that caused you to feel rejected. When you think of that person, you feel rejected again, then you get angry.

- A memory of something that happened that caused you to feel disappointed. You think of the memory, feel disappointed, and then get angry.

- A memory of yourself doing something that resulted in a personal loss. You felt stupid, then you got angry.

NOTE: Many of your strongest angry feelings are the result of memory cues attached to bad things that happened to you in the past. If you have suffered severe trauma in the past, you may not be able to completely heal from anger and rage until you resolve the trauma. As you learned in Chapter 5, a trauma is something that happened that was so scary you don't even want to talk about it. It is strongly suggested that you use this skill to deal with trauma only with a professional counselor. If you are now in counseling, show this skill to your counselor. Ask your counselor to use this skill to help you with your trauma memories. A professional counselor should have experience working with cognitive methods and will understand how best to use the skills.

Special Skills for Dealing With Stubborn Memory Cues

Special Skill #1: Dealing with Very Bright Negative Memory Cues

Select one of the stubborn memory cues you listed, then follow the instructions below. You may have to close your eyes to do some of the steps. If you need to close your eyes, you may open them long enough to read the next step. With practice you will not need to look at the steps. You will be able to do this skill from memory.

This is a difficult skill, but an important one. Ideally, you should have someone read the steps to you, perhaps a counselor or your Pathways to Peace sponsor. Once you have mastered this skill, you will have a way to deal effectively with any memory cue that threatens to keep you stuck in anger and rage.

1. Imagine that your mind is like a DVD player and recorder. You can control all of the features with a remote pad. Your mental DVD player remote pad has all the normal features, plus some that are quite advanced. For example, it has two Zoom buttons. It has a Zoom In button and a Zoom Out button. You will find this advanced feature very helpful when you use Special Skill #1.

   The memory cue you want to change is an image on a DVD which is stored in your brain's media cabinet. Put this DVD in your player and press Play. Skip forward to the particular image on the DVD that keeps causing you to have feelings that trigger your anger. When you get to that particular image, press the Pause button on your DVD player and stop the movie. Now you will see only that particular image, the one that causes you bad feelings that trigger your anger. It will be frozen on the screen. Pay special attention to the size of the image.

2. How angry does the memory cue makes you feel? Circle your anger level on the 10-point scale, below.

    1   2   3   4   5   6   7   8   9   10

3. Remember, your DVD player has two Zoom buttons. One to zoom in and one to zoom out. So now press the Zoom Out button on your mental DVD player. Press it very quickly three times. Notice what it does to the size of the image? Of course. Pressing the Zoom Out button three times causes the image to look smaller and farther away. Notice the effect this has on your anger level? Because the image looks smaller and farther away, you now find it difficult to see the details of the image. Notice that the image has lost some of its brightness too. The image is now rather dull, isn't it? In fact, seen smaller and from farther away, the image, which once captured your attention so easily and so quickly when it popped into your mind and caused you to have strong angry feelings, isn't very interesting at all anymore, is it?

    You've pressed the Zoom Out button three times. Now check your anger level. Circle your anger level on the scale below.

    1   2   3   4   5   6   7   8   9   10

4. If your anger level is still more than 3, press the Zoom Out button three more times. Notice that the image looks even smaller now and even farther away. The image has lost more of its brightness too, hasn't it? Notice how seeing the image six times smaller and six times farther away, than it was to begin with, affects the way you feel? By now, your anger must have lost much of the intensity. Rate your anger on the 10-point scale.

    1   2   3   4   5   6   7   8   9   10

5. If your anger level is still more than 2, press the Zoom Out button three more times. Better yet, keep pressing the Zoom Out button over and over again. Watch the original image shrink and become smaller and smaller as it moves farther and farther away in the distance. Keep pressing the Zoom Out button until the original image becomes nothing but a tiny, dim unrecognizable point of light, and then simply disappears from view altogether. Now rate your anger level.

    1   2   3   4   5   6   7   8   9   10

6. Your anger level should now be no more than 2 on the scale. But just to make sure, repeat Step 5 three more times.

Now you have a special skill to use when your brain plays a DVD containing one of those stubborn visual images. You can use the steps under Special Skill #1 to stop yourself from going over the Falls. But you will need to spend some time practicing Special Skill #1, so that you will be able to do the skill quickly in different situations. You will need to become very good at using Special Skill #1.

Choose another stubborn memory cue from your list and use the six steps of Special Skill #1 to change the image that causes you to have a feeling that triggers your anger. With practice, you will soon be able to quickly use this skill any place, any time, with excellent results. You will notice that some of the stubborn memory cues will continue to reappear and give you trouble. But don't give up. Keep using Special Skill #1 every time the stubborn memory cue pops into your mind. If you do, the stubborn memory cue will eventually trouble you no more. It will continue to fade and become less and less interesting until, finally, your mind will simply pay little or no attention to that particular memory cue.

Special Skill #2: Dealing With Negative Self-Talk Cues

Chances are there are CD recordings in your mental media storage cabinet of negative things you say about yourself. These bothersome CDs play back automatically, especially during times of stress, and often act as anger cues. We'll call these CDs "negative self-talk cues." Sometimes your name is mentioned in the negative message on the CD. Let's say your name is Joe. When one of these CDs starts to play, you might hear statements like this: "Joe, you're really stupid! Joe, you're never going to get your life together—never!" These negative self-talk messages take many forms. Whatever form they take, the result is always the same. They make you feel powerless and then they trigger your anger. But you can use Special Skill #2 to overcome these negative self-talk CDs.

1.   Think of a negative self-talk mental CD that you sometimes hear playing inside your mind, triggering your anger. When the CD starts to play, rate your anger on the 10-point scale.

1   2   3   4   5   6   7   8   9   10

2.   Now press the Erase button on your mental CD player. Wait for the CD to replay. Now press the Erase button again.

Repeat Steps 1 and 2 and over until the negative message is erased altogether, or until you can barely hear the words. If this skill doesn't work for you, try this variation: Step 1 is the same. In Step 2 of the variation, press the Fast Forward button instead of Erase. Repeat Step 2 until the negative message plays back so fast you can no longer understand the message.

Special Skill #3: Learning to Change Your Posture, Breathing, and Voice

You have learned that your mental focus creates how you feel at any given time. You have learned that a negative mental focus causes you to have negative feelings, and that negative feelings trigger your anger. But the physical part of your whole self also plays a role in determining how you feel. Whether you feel happy or sad, calm or angry depends on three things connected to your physical body: your posture, your breathing, and your voice.

Your posture, along with how you breathe and use your voice, creates whatever emotional state you happen to be in at a given time. Every feeling you experience is connected to these three aspects of your body. You cannot stay angry unless you use your body, your breathing, and your voice in an angry way. When you are angry, this is what you do:

- You maintain a rigid posture.
- You breathe rapidly in your upper chest.
- You speak rapidly in a loud high-pitched voice.

This posture, breathing, and voice pattern creates your anger. This pattern sends a specific message to the brain. It tells the brain to make stimulating chemicals associated with angry behavior. It tells the brain to stimulate the glands to produce large amounts of adrenaline.

Normally you are not consciously aware of your posture or how you breathe and use your voice, but you can learn how to be aware of these three very important things. If you learn how to be consciously aware of these three parts of your behavior, you will have a powerful way to change how you feel.

MESSAGE FROM FRANK

I'm Frank, from Little Rock. I'm seventeen years old. I thought this skill was too simple to work. I thought everything had to be complicated. Talk about limiting beliefs! But I tried it and found out that it worked. Changing my posture, my breathing, and my voice is the easiest way to change a bad feeling and to get out of the river. It's the fastest way too. It's an easy skill to learn, but you have to remember to do it. You have to try to use the skill every time you have a feeling that triggers your anger. After a while, it becomes automatic. At first, I took it one piece at a time. I started by paying attention to my breathing. Before, whenever I had a feeling that triggered my anger, like frustration or disappointment, I breathed real fast and high up in my chest. Now, when I have a trigger feeling, I tell myself to slow down my breathing and to breathe from my belly, not up in my chest.

After I got good at changing my breathing, then I started paying attention to my posture, too. Now I tell myself to relax my posture. Then I started paying attention to how I was using my voice. I found that just changing my breathing was often enough. When I changed my breathing, I found my posture and voice usually changed, too. I'm good at using this skill now. I can do it fast, and I can do it anywhere I happen to be. At home, in school—anywhere. Sometimes I don't even have to think about it. Something happens or I think about something that makes me have a feeling that triggers my anger, and my body just changes and the anger goes away.

Frank

Changing your posture, breathing, and voice changes how you feel. Follow the instructions below. When you feel angry:

- **First:** relax your posture—lean to one side, or sit down.
- **Second:** slow down your breathing—breathe more deeply, down in your belly.
- **Third:** speak more slowly, more softly, and use a deeper tone.

Changing your posture, breathing, and voice in the way described above will change how you feel. It will make you feel more relaxed and calm. It sends a different message to the brain. It tells the brain to stop making chemicals associated with angry behavior and tells it to start making chemicals associated with relaxation instead. Making these changes in your posture, breathing pattern, and voice thus interrupts the anger process.

· ·

SELF-TEST

1. Your mental focus determines how you feel. What you do with your body also plays a role in how you feel.

TRUE   FALSE

2. Describe how you use your posture, your breathing, and your voice when you are angry.

    Posture: _____
    Breathing: _____
    Voice: _____

3. There are three steps to changing how you feel by changing your posture, your breathing, and your voice. Describe the three steps to change your angry feelings.

    First: _____
    Second: _____
    Third: _____

· ·

Special Skill #3: Think of Something Funny That You Have Seen

In Chapter 12, you learned how to use a humorous DVD or a humorous CD to interrupt the anger process. Now you will learn another skill which takes advantage of the power of humor.

Did you ever see someone do something funny that made you laugh till you thought you couldn't stop laughing? If you have heard or seen something that funny, then you have at your fingertips a powerful way to deal with anger triggers.

In her message in the sidebar, Ellie describes an excellent way to use humor to interrupt anger. But as she points out, she had to be in cell phone range of the person she wanted to call, and the person she called had to be available. But, like Ellie, you can also use humorous things that actually happened.

The first step to using this special skill is to recall a time in the past when you saw a funny thing happen, something that made you laugh out loud. It is stored on a mental DVD somewhere in your media cabinet. Sort through your cabinet until you find it. Found it? Good. Put that DVD in your player. Don't press Play just yet.

MESSAGE FROM ELLIE

My name is Ellie. I had a bad problem with anger. I've been in recovery, now, for over a year, just since I turned seventeen. Now I'm doing a lot better. Early in my recovery, I found out how much humor could help. I had a friend named Jill. She knew I was addicted to anger and was trying to change my angry behavior. She knew a million jokes and was good at telling them. I thought I could make good use of Jill's skills. I figured I could call her when I was triggered, and ask her to tell me a joke. I thought the humor would act as an anchor to yank me out of the river. I told Jill about my idea, and she agreed to help. From then on, whenever I felt triggered, I'd call her and yell, "Tell me a joke. Quick!" It worked even better than I thought it would, even when I was in whitewater right down near the brink of the Falls. The only problem was sometimes I was out of range with my cell phone, or out of minutes. Also, sometimes Jill wasn't available. All I'd get was her message service. When that happened, I'd think of something funny I'd heard or seen in the past and use that. And you know what? It usually worked.

Ellie

Okay, now recall a time in the past when you were angry and your anger was about a level 5 or 6 on a 10-point scale. Continue thinking about that angry memory until it reaches 5 or 6. When your anger reaches that level, press Play on your mental DVD player and start watching the DVD of that funny thing you once saw that makes you laugh out loud whenever you think of it. Watch the recording of that funny thing for two or three minutes, then press Pause and check your anger level. If your anger level is still more than a 3, press Play again and watch the recording of the funny thing you saw for five more minutes. If your anger level isn't down to 2 or less, try watching the recorded memory of the funny thing that happened for another five minutes or so. If your anger still hasn't gone down, then try one of the other skills you have learned so far in this book.

Here is a variation on this skill. Recall the funny thing that you saw which made you laugh out loud. Then write down a few sentences on an index card that describes what you saw. Carry the card with you or record the funny event on your MP3 player. That way, when you see or hear something, or remember seeing or hearing something that triggers your anger, you could read what you wrote or listen to the recording. Reading or listening to your description would help you to recall more easily the entire memory of the funny thing you saw which you want to use to interrupt your anger.

Special Skill #4: Think of Something You Have Heard That Made You Laugh Out Loud

Have you ever heard someone say something so funny that it made you laugh out loud? Of course you have. Everybody has at least a few memories like this recorded on CDs and stored somewhere in their media cabinet. The first step to using this skill is to recall a time in the past when you heard a funny remark or story that made you laugh out loud. It is stored on a mental CD somewhere in your media cabinet. Sort through your CDs until you find it. Put the CD with the funny thing you heard into your CD player. Don't press Play just yet.

Next, recall a time in the past when you were angry and your anger was about a level 5 or 6 on a 10-point scale. Continue thinking about that angry memory until it reaches level 5 or 6. When your anger reaches that level, press Play on your mental CD player and start listening to the CD of that funny thing you heard that makes you laugh out loud whenever you think of it. Listen to the CD recording of that funny thing for two or three minutes, then press Pause and check your anger level. If your anger level is still more than a 3, press Play again and listen to the CD for five more minutes. If your anger level isn't down to 2 or less, try listening to the CD for another five minutes or so. If your anger still hasn't gone down, then try one of the other skills you have learned so far in this book.

Here is a variation on Special Skill #4. Recall the funny thing that made you laugh out loud. Write down on an index card or in your journal a few sentences that describe it. Next time you hear something, or recall hearing something that triggers your anger, read what you wrote. Reading your brief written description will help you to recall more easily the entire memory of the funny thing that made you laugh, which you want to use to interrupt your anger.

Aggression Versus Assertiveness

When you are aggressive, that means you are hostile. It means you are saying or doing something that is harmful or

---

MESSAGE FROM HOWARD

My name is Howard. I've got a problem with anger and it has cost me a lot, even though I'm only sixteen years old. I hurt a lot of people with my angry words and angry behavior. I feel bad about it now. I couldn't tell when I was acting aggressively or assertively. I couldn't tell the difference. I thought that as long as I wasn't hitting someone or throwing something, I was being assertive. When I used words to threaten people, I didn't know that counted as aggression. When I used my posture to scare somebody, I didn't count that as aggression either. Same with gestures. If I raised my fist at somebody or flipped them off, I didn't count that as aggression. Most of the time I didn't even know when I was using

---

potentially harmful. Angry words are aggressive words. Angry behavior is aggressive behavior.

Examples of Aggressive Statements:

- You're stupid!
- You don't know what you're talking about!
- You better stop that right now—or else!
- If you say that again, you'll be sorry!

Examples of Aggressive Behavior:

- Assuming a threatening posture
- Jabbing at someone's chest with your finger
- Throwing something or breaking something
- Hitting or kicking something or someone
- Shoving or pushing someone

You need to replace aggressive statements and behaviors with assertive statements and behaviors.

Write down one example of an aggressive statement you have used.

_____

_____

Write down one example of aggressive behavior you have used.

_____

_____

Special Skill #5: How to Be Assertive

When you are assertive, it means you are making a statement. It means you are declaring something. It means you are saying something or doing something that makes a statement about how you feel. Assertive statements and behaviors are non-threatening. They do not scare people or put people on the defensive.

threatening words or postures. I mean I wasn't aware when I was doing that, because I was so used to behaving that way. But I had to learn to be aware of my words and my posture. I had to learn to be aware of the way I said things too. I practiced listening to my own voice. I tuned into how loudly I spoke and I paid attention to the tone of my voice. I learned to pay attention to my posture. I found out I sounded and looked pretty aggressive even when I wasn't consciously trying to be. When I was just trying to be assertive, I spoke too loud. My voice tone was too high. I spoke too fast. Then I began to change how I spoke so that I wouldn't sound so aggressive. I noticed I often stood too close to the people I was talking to. And I leaned too far forward. Then I changed how I used my posture, and that made me look less aggressive. I also noticed how I used my eyes. I saw I often made too much eye contact. I drilled other people's eyes with mine when I talked to them. So I stopped doing that so much. I learned how to break eye contact once in a while. Changing these things about how I talked and said things, and how I used my posture and gestures really helped my anger problem. It made me take notice of my angry feelings, which was how I felt most of the time. I began to be less angry because I had less inner tension. I found out I got what I wanted or needed more often when I acted assertive instead of aggressive. And I didn't have to pay consequences either—hey, I haven't been in detention in almost six months!

Howard

Assertive Statements

An assertive statement will let the listener know what you need or how you feel, and it will usually not cause the person to react in a negative way.

Examples of Assertive Statements:

- What you said made me feel hurt.
- What you said made me feel rejected.
- What you said made me feel disappointed.
- What you did made me feel embarrassed.
- What you did made me feel disrespected.
- What you did hurt my self-esteem.

How to Use Your Voice When Making an Assertive Statement

Assertive statements require you to use your voice in a certain way. An assertive voice is a non-threatening voice, but not a wimpy voice. Keep these four guidelines in mind:

1. Use a strong voice, but not loud.
2. Speak clearly.
3. Speak at a normal rate, not too fast.
4. Use a lower voice tone, not high-pitched.

Assertive Behaviors

Assertive behaviors require you to use your body in a certain way. Use an assertive posture with assertive gestures. Assertive posture with assertive gestures are non-threatening, but they are not submissive. Keep these four guidelines in mind when you are using assertive behaviors:

1. Maintain an alert posture, but not tense.
2. Make slower gestures, not quick, abrupt gestures.
3. Make relaxed eye contact; don't stare.
4. Maintain a neutral expression; don't smile or scowl.

Examples of Assertive Behaviors:

- Answering a question using a calm, clear voice
- Raising your voice slightly to emphasize disappointment
- Making eye contact and leaning forward slightly when telling someone you feel frustrated

. . . .

SELF-TEST

1. Write down three examples of assertive statements. Make them different from the examples given.

    1. _____

    2. _____

    3. _____

2. Write down three examples of assertive behaviors different from those given on the previous page.

    1. _____

    2. _____

    3. _____

. . . .

Special Skill #6: When Possible, Take a Brief Respite When You Feel Overwhelmed

You are learning new ways to respond to triggers. But sometimes you will feel like you are on trigger overload. Things can pile up until you begin to feel overwhelmed. At such times you might need to take a brief respite. To take a respite means to take time out. It means taking a break from a stressful situation, one of those situations that lead to triggering feelings. For example, a situation that causes you to feel frustrated or anxious for a long period of time.

Taking a respite is not running away. It is taking time out—time out to think things through, time out to calm down. Sometimes you may need to get out of the situation entirely for a while.

Sometimes a brief respite will allow you to come back later and deal more effectively with the stress that caused you to feel so overwhelmed. You could go away for an hour or two. You could take a walk or go to a movie. You could go and talk with your Pathways to Peace sponsor (you will learn about Pathways to Peace sponsors later in this guidebook).

A respite is not defeat. Taking a respite is another choice; it is another anchor to throw on shore, another way to get out of the river. You could add "respite" to your list of choices.

NOTE: This skill does not mean that you can bolt out of your classroom or out of your home whenever you feel like it. Before you take a brief respite or a longer one, tell your mom or dad, or legal guardian what you are doing and why. Get their permission to go. Tell them when you plan to return. If your mom or dad or guardian tells you not to leave, then stay where you are and use the other skills you have learned so far in the book. Also, do not leave your classroom without first asking permission from the teacher. If your teacher says "no," then stay where you are and use your other anger management skills. Remember, you still have to be accountable.

. . . .

SELF-TEST

1. What does it mean to take a brief respite?

2. If you need to take a brief respite, where would you go?

3. Taking a brief respite means defeat.

TRUE   FALSE

4. Before leaving your house or leaving your classroom, you should first ask permission.

TRUE   FALSE

5. If your mom or dad, or your teacher says "No," you should stay where you are and use your other anger management skills.

TRUE   FALSE

. . . .

Special Skill #7: Go to a Pathways to Peace Meeting

You may already be involved in the Pathways to Peace program. That might be how you came to have this guidebook. You can learn more about the Pathways to Peace program in Appendix A, in the back of this workbook. You will want to take advantage of this self-help program. It will help assure your success in recovering from your anger habit.

Successful Pathways to Peace members attend meetings regularly. The meetings help you learn to deal with triggers. They help you learn the Pathways to Peace Principles. The Pathways to Peace Principles are behavior guidelines that help you manage your anger and stay out of trouble. Of course you will want to read the rest of this book, *Managing Teen Anger and Violence*. But, ideally, you will also attend Pathways to Peace meetings in order to reinforce what you learn from this book. Pathways to Peace members offer each other support, understanding, and friendship. Pathways to Peace program members know what you are going through.

To find out whether there is a Pathways to Peace group in your area, call the Pathways to Peace Inc. toll-free number: 1-800-775-4212. If no one answers the phone, leave a message along with your phone number, and someone will get back to you within 24 hours. Or send an email to Pathways to Peace; the email address is transform@netsync.net. If there is no Pathways to Peace support group in your area, you will be given free information on how to start a Pathways to Peace teen group. Appendix B gives detailed information on how to start a Pathways to Peace support group and how to facilitate a group.

Special Skill #8: Establish and Use an Empowerment Cue

You have learned that you have an anger habit. You know that you learned your anger habit by repeating angry behavior over and over. This kind of learning process is sometimes called "conditioning." It is an example of "stimulus/response conditioning." The term "stimulus/response conditioning" was first used by Russian scientist Ivan Pavlov to explain how human beings and many other living things learn certain behaviors. Your anger problem is a result of learning to behave in an angry way, more or less automatically, when your brain links up with a cue that results in a negative feeling which then triggers your anger.

You have also learned that the trigger for your anger habit is a negative feeling, such as fear or frustration. The negative feeling is what fires off the anger process and plunges you into the river. The negative feeling is the trigger. The trigger is the stimulus part of the stimulus/response conditioning process which you used to learn your anger habit. The trigger stimulates your anger process, or program, to go into action. The response to the stimulus is your angry behavior.

There is another part to the conditioning process: the reward. You will not form a habit unless you are rewarded for the behavior. A reward is a feeling of pleasure. The reward for your angry behavior is the feeling of power you experience when you get angry. The feeling of power is the pleasure you feel when you use anger; it is the reward.

Each time you use anger and are rewarded by feeling powerful, your habit grows stronger. It is reinforced. When a habit is reinforced often enough, it becomes so strong that even when you use anger to feel powerful and it does not work, you will still want to repeat the same behavior. If you were not rewarded often when you first started using anger to feel powerful, you would not have developed a problem with anger—the learning would have been unsuccessful. If you had experienced more pain than pleasure when you first used anger to respond to a negative feeling, you would have stopped using angry behavior as often, and your angry behavior would not have become a habit. But you were rewarded with pleasure more often than having painful consequences, so you learned how to use anger often. Over a period of time your anger got out of hand, so that now you are having very painful consequences because of your angry behavior. The consequences have become so painful, in fact, and the pleasure so weak by comparison, that you have decided to stop your angry behavior and learn new ways to feel powerful. That is one of the reasons you have a desire to change your behavior.

Now you want to change. You want to recover from your anger habit and stop behaving violently. You want to stop hurting people and damaging things. But now you find yourself saying and doing angry things even though you have sincerely promised to stop angry behavior. That is the nature of a habit. It is the nature of an addiction. You know you have developed a habit or are addicted to something when you find yourself doing the behavior even when you have decided not to do it.

The process of how to establish and use empowerment cues takes advantage of the same stimulus/response conditioning process that your brain used to create your anger habit. You will learn how to develop a new habit. The new habit you will learn is called recovery from your anger habit.

You have already learned something about anger cues. You learned that anger cues are signals that cause negative feelings and that negative feelings trigger your anger. Now you will learn about another class of cues: positive cues. Positive cues help you feel empowered, instead of feeling powerless.

A positive cue helps you interrupt negative feelings, such as disappointment or fear, which are anger triggers. There are three main types of positive cues: positive cues you can see, positive cues you can hear, and positive cues you can feel.

Positive Cues You Can See

A photo or a visual memory of someone you like and admire is a positive empowerment cue. Here are two examples:

- A favorite family member
- A favorite teacher

When you look at a photo or recall from memory an image of a person you like and admire, you probably end up feeling in some way empowered. You may end up feeling excited, for example. Or you may end up feeling confident. That's because you like and admire the person represented by the image you have of him or her. You have given that person hero status. So when you see or recall an image of your hero, it causes you to have strong positive feelings. If you relate to your heroes strongly enough, you will end up with strong positive feelings whenever you see or recall their images. In other words, seeing or recalling their images will cause you to feel empowered.

Before reading further, take a minute right now to list at least two people who make you feel empowered whenever you look at or recall their images. For future reference, circle the number next to the one who makes you feel the most strongly empowered when you look at or recall that particular image.

1. _____

2. _____

3. _____

Positive Cues You Can Hear

The sound of a certain song or piece of music that excites you very much in a good way is an empowerment cue that you can hear. Listening to exciting music or remembering a piece of exciting music makes some people feel empowered. Here are some examples of positive empowerment cues you can hear:

- Your favorite rock song
- Ocean waves crashing on shore
- A certain non-violent rap poem

Before going to the next section, write down at least three positive sounds that cause you to feel empowered when you hear them.

1. _____

2. _____

3. _____

For future reference circle the number next to the one which makes you feel the most strongly empowered when you hear it or recall what it sounds like in memory.

Positive Cues You Can Feel

Any object you can hold which gives you a positive feeling when you touch it is an empowerment cue you can feel. Here are some examples of positive empowerment cues you can feel:

- A lucky coin
- A religious object (such as a cross or crucifix)
- A magic amulet (sometimes called a good luck charm)
- A toy you had as a child

Before reading further, stop and list three things that make you have positive feelings when you touch them. For future reference, circle the number next to the one that makes you feel the most empowered.

1. _____

2. _____

3. _____

Establishing an Empowerment Cue on Your Wrist

One of the disadvantages of using an object such as a coin, religious object, or amulet as a positive cue is that you may lose the object. Using the technique described below, however, you can learn how to connect a positive cue to a specific location on your body, such as your wrist. The advantage of this kind of positive cue is that you cannot lose the cue. It is customary to place the cue on the wrist. Once established, the cue can be easily used whenever you need it.

This empowerment cue technique is not as strange as it may, at first, sound. Most people find this technique fascinating as well as useful. They are often amazed at how well it works, and they grow to appreciate the feeling of self-empowerment the technique gives them.

Follow the steps below:

1. Decide on which wrist you want to establish the cue. If you are right-handed, the left wrist is usually the better choice. If you are left-handed, then placing the positive cue on the right wrist would be better.

2. Next, recall a memory of a time you had a strong positive feeling. For example, when you felt confident or proud. Both of these are examples of positive feelings that make you feel empowered. In your imagination, see, hear, and feel everything that went on when you had that strongly positive feeling.

> **MESSAGE FROM SEAN**
>
> *My counselor helped someone connect a strong positive cue on his wrist as part of a demonstration in a group. She helped him establish a strong empowerment cue on his wrist that was connected to a memory of when he'd had a real strong positive feeling. He was right-handed, so she helped him place the cue on his left wrist. Then she had the dude think of a time when he was real angry. He had a serious problem with anger and rage. In fact, he'd been in a detention center because of what he did to someone once when he was real angry. So he had no problem remembering something he connected up with intense anger! He focused on the memory of that time. I was watching him real close. His breath got real fast and ragged. He was breathing real high up in the chest and his posture was rigid. He looked like a board with arms and legs. The muscles in his face and neck quivered. His face got bright red. The rest of the group got uneasy, watching. So did I. Then the counselor told him to fire the stimulus. At first, nothing happened. He kept squeezing the cue point, as we all kept watching. Slowly, things started to change. After about half a minute, he returned to normal. The anger was gone. He had a sort of relaxed smile on his face. Did you ever see that old movie called Dr. Jekyll and Mr. Hyde? It was like watching crazy Mr. Hyde transform himself back into gentle Dr. Jekyll.*
>
> *Sean*

When the positive feeling is at its strongest, grasp your wrist firmly using your thumb and index finger. Squeeze your wrist firmly for 15-20 seconds, then let go.

3. Recall again the event that gave you the strong positive feeling. As soon as the positive feeling reaches its strongest point once more, use your thumb and forefinger to connect the cue again. Use the same amount of pressure as before, at the exact same spot. Hold for 15-20 seconds, then let go. Establishing the cue again reinforces the original cue. The process should be repeated as often as needed in order to establish a very strong positive cue. The cue must be strong—at least an 8 on a scale from 1 to 10. Otherwise the stimulus will end up being too weak. The nervous system will fail to link up the internal image with the response. You must make sure to reset the cue point at the same spot applying the same amount of pressure with the finger and thumb each time you reset it. If the same location is not used or if the pressure is varied, the brain will get different messages and the link-up between the cue and the memory of the original event may not take place. At best, it will end up diluted and weak.

4. This is the testing step. In order to make sure the cue is strong enough, you must test the cue. In order to test the cue, recall a time when you felt angry. When the angry feeling is at its strongest, fire the positive cue by squeezing the cue point on the wrist, using exactly the same pressure as was used to establish the positive cue in the first place. The cue point should be held for at least 30 seconds. You may have to wait a little longer before letting go, depending on the strength of the cue and on the strength of the competing anger trigger. Generally, 30 to 60 seconds is adequate. At the end of 30 to 60 seconds, you should begin to notice a change. For example, your breathing should slow down. You may also notice a decreased heart rate or pulse rate. You will begin to feel less angry.

Using an Aversion Cue

In order to make major behavior changes, it is useful to have both the carrot and the stick. An empowerment cue is the carrot. When used, an empowerment cue leads to a pleasurable result. It makes you have positive feelings. An aversion cue leads to a different result. It makes you have the opposite kind of feeling—pain. An aversion cue is the stick. An empowerment cue is connected to a memory of a time in the past which you associate with strong pleasure. An aversion cue is connected to a memory of a time in the past which you associate with intense pain.

Once established, the aversion cue can be used any time you feel a strong desire to use anger or violence. When you fire the cue, you will re-experience the same painful feelings that you felt at the time of the original experience.

Using your aversion cue will cause you to stop and think, "Do I want to use verbal or physical violence in this situation and end up with that consequence again? Do I want to put myself through that pain again?"

The process used to establish an aversion cue is essentially the same as that which is used to establish an empowerment cue. It is always best to establish the aversion cue on the hand opposite the one on which the empowerment cue is located. If the empowerment cue was established on the wrist of the right hand, then the aversion cue should be established on the left hand. Specifically, the aversion cue should be established on the large knuckle of the index finger of the left hand. This makes it easier for the person using the skill to mentally separate the two cues, so that there is no confusion regarding the use of the two cues.

To establish an aversion cue for the purpose of interrupting the anger process, follow the steps below.

1. Recall from memory a time in the past when you experienced an anger trigger and anticipated experiencing a strong feeling of pleasure as a result of using anger, but ended up feeling intense emotional or physical pain, or both, instead. Write it down so that you can refer back to it.

   Rather than feeling powerful, the event you recalled from memory and wrote down caused you to lose something of value and you ended up feeling even more powerless. Maybe on that occasion, you were sent to detention and lost your freedom. Maybe you were humiliated in front of your friends—how painful is that? Make sure the experience you wrote down was so bad, you ended up saying to yourself, "I just have to find a different way to respond to anger triggers! I don't want to lose more than I've already lost, and I don't want to feel any more pain than I've already felt!"

2. At the peak, when you are re-experiencing at its strongest the painful feeling of the original event, firmly squeeze the large knuckle on your left index finger using the thumb and index finger of your right hand. Maintain firm pressure for approximately 30 seconds, then let go.

3. Now test the aversion cue. Think of something that would generate a craving to use anger. At the peak, when you feel the strongest craving to use anger, squeeze the aversion cue. Be sure to use the same pressure at the exact same location on the large knuckle of the index finger on the left hand. When the feelings of the aversion cue start, you will find yourself wanting to stop the anger. If the craving to use anger has been interrupted, you may assume you have succeeded in establishing the aversion cue.

4. If the craving is still active, reestablish a stronger aversion cue and re-test. Continue using the skill until you have established a stimulus that will interrupt any anger cue.

SELF TEST

1. Now that you have learned how to establish a strong aversion cue, make a list of 6-10 major anger cues. Take each cue, one at a time, and extinguish them using your aversion cue.

. . . .

PART FOUR

Changing Your Mindset

CHAPTER FIFTEEN

Identify and Change Your Beliefs and Values

This chapter begins the last part of the workbook. It represents a whole new phase of healing from your anger habit. Until now, most of the focus has been on helping you change your behavior. Changing your behavior is the work of your conscious mind. You had to use your conscious mind in order to acquire the skills you have learned. This chapter, and the ones to follow, focus on helping you heal at a deeper level. You will learn how to make changes in your *subconscious* mind, and that will make your healing more complete.

You have already learned about the power of your subconscious mind. You now know that your anger habit is stored in your subconscious mind, and that other automatic habits and automatic programs are also stored in your subconscious mind. In fact, your subconscious mind is a vast storehouse and holds information about everything you have ever seen, heard, tasted, smelled, or felt. Your subconscious mind holds all of your memories. Your memories are recorded on mental DVDs and CDs and are stored in your mental media cabinet. Remember the metaphor?

But your subconscious mind stores other things in its vast depths. Your subconscious mind holds all of the higher parts of your whole self. It holds all of your beliefs, your values and goals, your sense of mission, and your feelings of spirituality. These are the powerful parts of your whole self. These parts represent your higher self, and they are what actually determines your behavior. Accessing your subconscious mind will make it easier to change your angry behavior, and it will make it easier to keep your behavior changed.

Changing at the deeper subconscious level of the whole self will take you to a higher level as a human being. You will be transformed.

Beliefs

Excessive anger isn't just a behavior problem. In fact, angry behavior is a symptom. It is a sign of a belief problem. You could even say that your beliefs are responsible for your anger problem, because your beliefs run your anger habit.

What Are Beliefs?

Beliefs are the ideas that you have formed about yourself and your world. You may regard your beliefs as true, right, or good, but your beliefs are *not* facts. Beliefs are *not* things. They are strong feelings. Most of the time you are not aware of your beliefs, because they are stored in your subconscious mind. They are the DVDs and CDs that are stored way back in the dusty rear part of your mental media cabinet—DVDs and CDs that you frequently play, but you aren't aware of it.

Beliefs are the ideas that guide your life. Your beliefs give your life direction and meaning. A belief is a feeling you have about whether something is true or false, good or bad, or right or wrong.

There are two kinds of beliefs: positive beliefs and negative beliefs.

Positive Beliefs

Positive beliefs empower you. They open doors of possibility and they support you. They make you feel you are worthwhile. They make you regard other people as worthwhile. They make you feel the world is worthwhile.

Positive beliefs tend to brighten your outlook. They give you confidence by helping you see the future in an optimistic light.

Positive beliefs make you feel good about yourself, others, and the world. Positive beliefs cause positive feelings, and positive feelings keep you out of the river of anger and rage.

Negative Beliefs

Negative beliefs are toxic. They act like a poison. Negative beliefs limit you. They dis-empower you. They slam shut doors of possibility. They work against you by making you feel your life is not worthwhile. They make you feel other people are not worthwhile, and they make you feel the world is not worthwhile. Negative beliefs cause you to make decisions and to act in ways that harm others and yourself. That is why negative beliefs are toxic.

Negative beliefs tend to darken your outlook. They increase your fear and take away your confidence, by causing you to see the future in a pessimistic light.

Negative beliefs make you feel bad about yourself, other people, and the world. Negative beliefs cause negative feelings. Negative feelings, as you already know, are feelings that trigger your anger habit.

How Did You Acquire Your Beliefs?

As you found out in Part I of this book, you were not born with your beliefs. You acquired your beliefs from your parents, from your teachers, and from your peers. You learned them from the mass media. You learned some of your beliefs as a result of things that happened to you. Since beliefs are learned, that means you can let go of old beliefs and learn new ones. But sometimes it is hard to let go of old beliefs, even when they no longer work for you.

Why You Need to Change Your Beliefs

You know how important it is to stay out of the river and away from the Falls. You have learned some skills to change your behavior. You have learned how to get out of the river using your skills. You have learned how to change your breathing, your posture, and your voice to stop the anger process quickly. You have learned to use other skills, too, to stop yourself from going over the Falls again. Those skills help you avoid negative results.

But you need to make major belief changes too. For example, what if you continue to believe that anger is a good way to show how you feel? What if you continue to believe that anger means power? Those are the kinds of beliefs that have kept you stuck in your anger habit. Those are the beliefs that keep you in the river. To fully heal from your anger problem, you need to change your character.

Since your beliefs are a major part of your character, you need to give up the negative beliefs that keep you stuck and replace them with beliefs that support your recovery. The following true account dramatically illustrates how much power beliefs have in a person's life.

> A man was asked to take part in an experiment about the power of belief. The experiment used hypnosis. The man was hypnotized and went into a deep trance. A trance is like being very relaxed but still awake. While the man was in the trance, he was told he would be touched on the arm with a piece of hot metal but was actually touched with a piece of ice. A blister formed at the point on his arm where he believed he was touched with hot metal!

Beliefs have a powerful influence in your life. The power of your beliefs affects all other levels of recovery from anger, even the biological level.

Beliefs and Anger

Your anger habit is powered by negative beliefs. Negative beliefs are like the gasoline that runs the car. Stop and think about it. Would you have developed an anger habit if you hadn't believed anger was a good way to change how you feel?

You used anger and violence to hurt people. You hurt them physically or emotionally, or both. You could not have continued hurting people if you hadn't believed it was okay. Think about it. Your beliefs are the foundation for your anger habit. Your beliefs are the concrete upon which your anger habit is built, and it is your beliefs that have kept you stuck in anger.

In order to heal from anger and rage, you need to identify the beliefs you hold about anger that keep you stuck. Then you need to change those beliefs. You need to change your beliefs about the meaning of anger. You need to give up the belief that anger means pleasure and, instead, adopt the belief that anger means pain. Changing your basic beliefs about anger will make it easier to stop your angry behavior, because *your beliefs cause your behavior.*

. . . .

SELF-TEST

1. Changing your behavior is the work of your conscious mind.

    TRUE   FALSE

2. Your anger isn't just a behavior problem. It is also a belief problem.

    TRUE   FALSE

3. All of the parts of your higher self, including your beliefs, are stored in your subconscious mind.

    TRUE   FALSE

4. You could say your beliefs run your anger program.

    TRUE   FALSE

5. Beliefs are facts.

    TRUE   FALSE

6. Beliefs are like strong feelings.

    TRUE   FALSE

7. Negative beliefs tend to take away your power.

    TRUE   FALSE

8. Your beliefs affect every part of your whole self, including the physical part.

    TRUE   FALSE

9. You want to change your angry behavior and are learning how to change it. Explain in a few words what will happen if you do not also change your beliefs.

. . . .

How to Change Beliefs About Anger That Keep You Stuck

First, you need to identify the beliefs you hold about anger that keep you stuck. Look at the list of beliefs below. Some of them, perhaps, will be familiar. Circle the beliefs that you hold to be true.

Anger means power.

People respect me when I'm angry.

I was born with an anger problem.

I can't change my angry behavior.

If I stop using anger, people will take advantage of me.

If I stop using anger, I'll lose respect.

Chances are, you have other beliefs that keep you stuck in the anger process. Take a minute to write down some other beliefs you hold about anger that keep you stuck. List at least three.

1. _____

2. _____

3. _____

Now pick a negative belief from your list and make a decision to change it. Recognize the negative belief for what it is: a limitation. That negative belief stands in the way of permanently changing behaviors that have caused harm to other people and to yourself. You could even plug the negative belief you want to change into the motivation strategy you learned in Chapter 6.

I have made a decision to change the following belief:

_____

_____

Now think of a positive belief you want to adopt to replace the negative one. You may have targeted the belief "Anger means power," as the one you want to change. Now you might write down "I can learn how to feel powerful without using anger and violence," as the new belief to take the place of the old negative belief.

Examples of beliefs that will help you change old patterns of anger and rage:

I can learn new ways to feel powerful without using anger and rage.

I can learn how to gain respect without using violence and intimidation.

Anger means personal pain and pain for people I care about.

This is the new belief I want to replace the old negative belief:

_____

_____

Now write down three things you've already lost because of negative beliefs about anger and rage. Examples: loss of freedom, loss of school grade advancement, loss of friends.

Three things I have lost due to my negative beliefs about anger:

1. _____

2. _____

3. _____

Now write down three potential future losses you will suffer if you continue to hold the negative belief. Examples: spend time in a detention center (maybe go to prison), lose the chance to go to college, more rejection by others.

Three things I will lose in the future if I don't let go of the negative belief:

1. _____

2. _____

3. _____

Write down three specific benefits you know you will gain by changing that negative belief. Examples: more freedom, finish high school, exciting new relationship.

Three ways I will benefit if I do change the belief:

1. _____

2. _____

3. _____

Recall the old negative belief that you want to change, and look at the losses you listed. Close your eyes and, using your imagination, visualize the three losses you've already suffered. Get in touch with the pain the losses have caused you. Look at the future losses you listed, and visualize yourself experiencing those future losses. Exactly how does that make you feel? Spend at least three minutes on this step.

How I feel about my past losses:

_____

_____

_____

_____

_____

_____

_____

How I will feel in the future if I do not change that belief:

_____

_____

_____

_____

_____

_____

_____

Now recall the new positive belief and look at the benefits list. Close your eyes and imagine the future benefits of replacing that old negative belief with the new positive belief. Notice how that will make you feel.

How the benefits of changing that negative belief will make me feel in the future:

_____

_____

_____

_____

_____

_____

_____

_____

The best time to go through this process is just before you go to sleep at night. For best results, repeat the process every night for a period of five to seven days. Then you can start another cycle using a different negative belief.

Acquiring Positive Beliefs About Yourself, Others, and the World

Positive beliefs are beliefs that make you feel good about yourself, about other people, and about the rest of the world. Positive beliefs are positive statements. Positive statements about yourself are called affirmations.

Positive Beliefs About Yourself

Read the positive beliefs listed below. They are affirmations about yourself. Write them on a card and read them to yourself every morning before you start your day and each night just before you go to sleep.

> *I am a worthwhile person.*
>
> *I deserve to be happy.*
>
> *I deserve love.*
>
> *I deserve respect.*
>
> *I have a special purpose for being alive.*

Make a list of other self-empowering positive beliefs or affirmations that will help you heal from your anger problem.

These are other self-empowering positive beliefs or affirmations I want to acquire:

_____

_____

_____

_____

_____

_____

_____

_____

If possible, record your self-empowering beliefs on a CD or on your iPod. Then listen to the recording several times a day for one month. Listening to the recording of your self-empowering beliefs several times a day will tell your subconscious mind that you really want your new beliefs to become a permanent part of your belief system.

Positive Beliefs About Others

It is important to hold positive beliefs about yourself. Positive beliefs about yourself help you to see yourself in a positive light and will make you less likely to do or say things that result in painful consequences. It is equally important to hold positive beliefs about others. Holding positive beliefs about other people will help you see them in a positive light and make you less likely to harm them with angry behavior.

Read the positive beliefs about others listed below. Circle the beliefs you already hold.

Most people are basically good.

Most people are willing to help you when you need their help.

Most people can be trusted.

Think of one or two other positive beliefs you now hold about others, and write them down.

_____

_____

_____

_____

List at least three positive beliefs you would like to hold about other people, but don't right now.

_____

_____

_____

_____

Positive Beliefs About the World and Your Relationship to It

It is important to have positive beliefs about yourself and others. You also need positive beliefs about the world and positive beliefs about how you fit into the world. Positive beliefs about the world and your relationship to the world will help you see the world in a more positive light. Positive beliefs about the world will brighten your mood. They will make you more optimistic. Negative beliefs about the world and your relationship to it will keep you stuck in your anger habit.

Look at the positive beliefs listed below and circle the beliefs you already hold:

The world is mostly a friendly place.

The world has meaning.

I am a meaningful part of the world.

I have an important part to play in the world.

List at least three other positive beliefs about the world and your relationship to the world that you would like to hold:

_____

_____

_____

Beliefs About Death

The fear of death weighs on the minds of all human beings, even those still in their teens. For some reason, people who have an anger problem often feel the weight of the fear of death more heavily. Intense fear of death may be one of the basic causes of your anger habit. Intense fear of any kind is a major anger trigger.

Intense fear of death is directly related to negative beliefs about death. Until you give up your negative beliefs about death, you will never be rid of the fear of death. Until the fear of death is put to rest, that intensely negative feeling will always be a major anger trigger.

Negative Beliefs About Death

Look at the negative beliefs about death listed below. Do you hold any of these beliefs? Circle the negative beliefs that you hold about death.

Death is the end; there is nothing after that.

Death is the final insult.

After the struggle, death is the reward.

Death is a time of punishment and pain.

Life has no purpose; death even less of a purpose.

Do you hold other negative beliefs about death? Write them down:

_____

_____

_____

_____

_____

Describe in a few words how your negative beliefs about death make you feel.

_____

_____

_____

Positive Beliefs About Death

Look at the positive beliefs about death listed below. Circle the ones you might already hold:

Death leads to greater growth.

Death is a great resting time.

The soul survives the death of the body.

This life is like a school. If I learn what I need to learn, I will go to a higher grade when I die.

List at least two positive beliefs about death you would like to hold:

_____

_____

_____

_____

Explain in a few words how positive beliefs about death would make you feel:

_____

_____

_____

_____

Values

You have learned how negative beliefs keep you stuck in the anger process, and you have learned how to let go of negative beliefs and form new positive beliefs. Now it is time to look at your values, because values also influence your behavior. Actually, there are two kinds of values: valued things and valued feelings.

Valued Things Versus Valued Feelings

Of course you value things. Who doesn't? You value the house you live in. You value money. You value your DVD player and your DVD collection, your CD player and CD collection. You value your iPod and your MP3s, and the programs you have stored on them. You value some of the people in your life. You value your friends, your girlfriend or boyfriend. You value your mother and father, or whomever may be helping you grow and develop. The things and people you value and treasure are vehicles that move you toward your valued feelings and away from painful feelings. Valued feelings are positive feelings, such as love or confidence. Painful feelings are negative feelings, such as fear or depression. Of course, as you now know, painful feelings (negative feelings) are anger triggers.

Valued Feelings

Freedom, security, and love are examples of valued feelings. This class of values is important to everybody. Psychologists talk about three feelings all human beings must have in order to be happy. Psychologist William Glasser calls them the "three A's of happiness." They are:

1. Achievement
2. Acceptance
3. Affection

When you are unhappy, it is because your valued feelings have not been satisfied.

When you are angry it is because you believe one of your valued feelings has been threatened or attacked.

Assume that freedom and power are two of your most valued feelings. Assume that having a bicycle to ride or a car to drive gives you strong feelings of freedom and power. Suppose someone attacks your bicycle or car by beating it with a hammer and slashing the tires with a knife. Suppose the attack on your bicycle or car made you violently angry. Your anger would not be the result of the attack on your bicycle or car. Your anger would be the result of an attack on the valued feelings your bicycle or car represents. It would be an attack on your feelings of freedom and power. Your brain would interpret the attack on your bicycle or car as an attack on your personal freedom and personal power.

Values, like beliefs, influence how you act, and they influence how you spend your time and energy. Earlier, you learned you are not born with a set of beliefs, nor are you born with a set of values. Values, like beliefs, are learned. As with your beliefs, you learned some of your values from teachers and peers. You learned some of your values from movies and books. But you learned most of your values from your parents, or from whomever your caregivers were during the first ten years of your life.

Your anger habit has caused you to use anger like a valued thing, the way drug addicts use drugs as valued things. You have used anger like a drug to get high. You have used anger as a vehicle to satisfy one of your most valued feelings—the feeling of power.

Now you understand that anger is not a good vehicle to move you toward a feeling of power. Now you know that using anger like a drug causes more pain than pleasure. It causes pain for others and for yourself. Now you know you need to find and use other vehicles to take you to your valued feelings. You need to find other ways to feel powerful. You need to find other ways to feel confident.

> ### MESSAGE FROM CHARLIE
>
> *My name is Charlie. I'm not looking for high fives by telling my story. I'm ashamed for what I did. I committed an assault. I got arrested and taken to the Detention Center. I felt a little afraid and a little ashamed as I was being led by the guard to the lockup. He took off the handcuffs outside the cell, and swung open the door. I went inside rubbing my wrists because they hurt. I looked around. A cot stood against the wall, a stained toilet over in the corner. No window. I heard the door creaking on the hinges. Then I heard the sound of metal crashing against metal when the guard slammed the steel door shut. All of a sudden, I realized what had just happened. I'd just lost my freedom—again! It wasn't until that moment that I understood just how much I valued my freedom. Then I went into a rage. Man, did I carry on.*
>
> *CHARLIE*

Identifying Your Positive Values

This exercise will help you become aware of your valued feelings. It will help you see how being aware of your values will have a positive effect on your commitment to heal from your anger habit.

For this exercise, you will need 15-20 small pieces of paper. Make them about 1 inch high by about 1½ inches long. Don't worry about making the pieces of paper exactly 1 inch by 1½ inches. That isn't important. Use a pencil so you can erase. You'll need a flat surface to work on. Follow the instructions closely.

Examples of Valued Feelings

Here is a list of some examples of valued feelings that you can use to get started.

Contribution	Acceptance
Freedom	Independence
Loved/Loving	Growth
Serenity	Safety
Accomplishment	Calmness
Security	Confidence
Affection	Connectedness
Health	Achievement
Peace	Being liked

Because your values are stored somewhere down inside your subconscious mind, you will need to do a deep search in order to find them. You can accomplish this by asking yourself the following questions:

1. ***How do I want to feel every day as I live my new anger-free lifestyle?***

Your first answer might be: "*Loved.* I want to feel loved every day of my life." Whatever your first answer is to this question, write it down on one of the pieces of paper. Write down whatever valued feeling comes to mind.

2. ***What other feeling is important to me?***

Your next answer might be, "I'd like to feel *excited* every day in whatever I do." Whatever your second answer may be, write it down on another piece of paper. In the beginning, don't bother trying to put your values in any kind of order. For now, just write them all down.

3. ***What other feeling is important to me?***

Your third answer might be "*Peaceful.* I want to feel peaceful, at least some of the time, every day." Whatever your third answer is, write it down on another piece of paper.

MESSAGE FROM DONNA

*My name is Donna. I'm from Cincinnati, and I have a bad anger problem. I'm almost seventeen. When I was full of anger and rage I had no idea what my values were. I found out later my most valued feeling was anger. I treated anger as though it was a positive value. I used anger and rage to get high on my own brain chemicals. I used anger to feel powerful. I used anger to feel accepted by my friends, and I used it to fight off fear. I wasn't aware, not consciously anyway, of how short-lived the anger high was. It came and went in just a few seconds. But finally I did become aware of how long the pain of the consequences lasted, and I became aware of how long the pain lasted for people I hurt. Like most teens with an anger problem, I hurt my family most. The awareness of the pain that my behavior caused myself and others helped me see how important it was to learn about my values. I found out I had some true values — some **positive** values. I found out I had some values I could use that didn't result in pain for others or for myself.*

Donna

Continue asking yourself the question, "What other feelings are important in my life?," until you have at least ten different feelings written down on ten different pieces of paper. Place them all on the pile with the others. Spend at least ten minutes on this part of the process.

Keep going until you cannot think of any more values. Then arrange your values according to what is most important to you. Here's how to arrange your values:

A. Pick up the pieces of paper that you wrote your values on. Take the first two pieces and place them face up on the table or floor.

B. Let's say the values written on those two pieces of paper are *love* and *freedom*, respectively. Ask yourself, "What is more important in my life, love or freedom?" If the answer is "love," place the piece of paper with the word *love* at the top in first position. Right underneath it, place the one with the word *freedom*.

C. Take the next piece of paper from the pile. Let's say the third one says, "respect." Ask yourself again, "What is more important in my life—love, freedom, or respect?" If the answer is, "Respect is more important to me than freedom, but love is still more important than respect," then you will know you need to place *respect* second between *love* and *freedom*.

D. Continue arranging and rearranging your values according to what you feel is most important. Use all the pieces of paper you wrote your values on.

E. Now look at the arrangement. Ask yourself, "Are there any changes I want to make?" Keep rearranging your values until you know they are in the proper order. You will know by how the arrangement looks, sounds, and feels. If you feel no need to change the arrangement, consider this part of the exercise complete.

Finding Your Values Breaking Point

There is one other important thing to learn about values. There is a *breaking point* somewhere within their order of importance. For you it could be at number six or seven, or maybe eight or nine. Whatever that place is for you, it is the point at which you would say, "Stop! You can't take that away from me! I can't live without that value!"

Here is how to find your breaking point. Start with the last value on your arrangement. Ask yourself, "If I had all of the other good feelings above this one on my list, could I get along okay without this value?" If the answer is "Yes," go to the next value up the ladder of importance and ask the same question. Keep asking, "If I had all the other good feelings above this one, could I get along okay without this value?" When you hear yourself say "No! Absolutely not!," that is your breaking point.

Your breaking point has one other important meaning. Your breaking point is the value you will most likely get angry about if you think someone or something is threatening that value. Whatever that value is, it will be threatened once in a while. That is just how things are, sometimes.

You must learn how to respond differently when any of your values are threatened.

Now you know exactly what your values are and which ones are most important to you. You can use this knowledge to help yourself focus more effectively on what you really want in your life, and what you want to avoid. You can use this knowledge to help yourself see more clearly why you want to stop using anger and rage once and for all.

Values and Choosing a Career

Knowing what your very highest values are can also help you decide what kind of career you should pursue. Generally, people who choose a career that reflects their highest values are happy and successful in their work. People who choose a career that is in conflict with their highest values often fail or end up unhappy in their work.

To illustrate, let's say your highest value is helping and that you have discovered that you get a lot of pleasure from helping other teens solve their problems. Now let's say that you choose a career as an automobile mechanic, maybe because you think you could make more money as a mechanic than you would as a school counselor. Naturally, there is nothing wrong with being an automobile mechanic. Many people who choose that career are highly successful and end up happy in their work. But knowing that helping—more specifically, helping other teens solve their problems—is your highest value, how would it make you feel to work on cars all day? For you, wouldn't it be a serious conflict of values? You could end up making a lot of money as a mechanic, especially if you opened your own repair shop. But how would you feel at the end of the workday? And how would that conflict of values affect your anger problem?

Values and Relationships

Knowing what your very highest values are can also help you decide who you really want to have in your life. Knowing what your highest values are can help you choose friends who share your values. Knowing what your highest values are can help you avoid costly mistakes when you choose someone with whom to have a closer relationship—a love relationship. Most friendships and most relationships which fail usually don't last because of *incompatible* values. For example, what if one of your highest values is adventure and the person with whom you are thinking of having a close relationship has security at the top of his or her list? You would certainly discover, maybe too late, that you and the other person have a serious *conflict of values*. The conflict of values could undermine your relationship from the start, no matter how much each of you try to make the relationship work. If the other person's highest values, say the top seven values, are quite different from yours, the relationship may never work out. It is also important to know that you will not be able to make the other person change his or her values to match up with yours. Because you are still young, you can change some of your own values, or change where they fall in their order of importance. But you will not be able to persuade another person to completely change or re-order their values.

Make a List of Your Values

Now copy the list of values that you wrote on the small pieces of paper on the form below, so you will have a permanent record of them. List your values in their proper order. Identify your cutoff value by placing a star (*) next to it.

My Valued Feelings

1. _____

2. _____

3. _____

4. _____

5. _____

6. _____

7. _____

8. _____

9. _____

10. _____

11. _____

12. _____

13. _____

14. _____

15. _____

16. _____

17. _____

18. _____

19. _____

20. _____

CHAPTER SIXTEEN

Your Life Mission and Spirituality

In this chapter you will learn the importance of identifying your life mission. You will be asked to write down your personal mission statement. Then you will learn how to use your mission statement to help you manage your anger.

What is Your Life Mission?

Your life mission is what you believe to be the meaning of your life. It is what you believe you were born to be and to do. It is what you believe to be the main reason that you are alive. Your life mission is what would be left of you if everything else that you find important about your life were taken away. It is what would make you want to go on living.

Your mission must benefit others as well as yourself. It must bring good into your life, and it must bring good into the lives of others. That is the nature of a life mission: to bring good into your life and into the lives of others. For persons with an anger problem, this is a useful belief.

It is useful to believe that you were born with a mission but have forgotten what it is. Now it is time to re-discover your mission. Re-discovering your life mission will be difficult because your mission, like your beliefs and your values, is buried deep inside your subconscious mind. Now you *must* resurrect it by pulling it back up into consciousness, the way the sun pulls flowers up from the earth in springtime.

It is useful to think of your mission not as a choice, but as a mandate. A mandate is something you cannot get out of doing. It is something you *must* do. Think of your life mission as something you must do. We are not talking about a detention center sentence. Your life mission isn't that kind of mandate. It isn't handed down by a school principal, a judge, or a probation officer. No outside agent has the power to mandate your life mission. Your life mission is sacred. It is, in fact, the most sacred part of your whole self. This most sacred part of your self is yours, and yours alone. Therefore when it comes to your life mission, you and only you can issue that mandate. So your life mission is a self-mandate.

Please read the statement below very carefully, because it is extremely important. Also, try to stay consciously aware of the words as you read the rest of this chapter.

> *People who lack conscious awareness of their mission and have lost many of the things they value are at high risk for losing the will to live.*

You have decided to change your angry behavior. You have studied your beliefs and have decided to change old beliefs about anger that have kept you stuck in angry behavior. You have sorted out your values and found your breaking point. Now you come to the next important step in your recovery from your anger habit. Now you need to discover your personal mission and then write it down.

Your mission statement is potentially your most powerful choice. One reason it is so powerful is that if you focus on your mission statement daily, it will help you stay out of the anger process, out of the Niagara River, most of the time. And

MESSAGE FROM FLOYD

*My name is Floyd. I'm a sixteen-year-old from Atlanta. I have a problem with anger. I had no idea I had a special purpose, a life mission. In fact, I was sure I didn't have a special purpose for being alive, and that no one else had a purpose either. Now I know that was one of the reasons I was so angry all the time. To me, my life and everybody else's were **meaningless**. Believing that, I couldn't make sense out of anything. Even good feelings didn't make sense to me, and I sure couldn't make sense out of the pain in my life. I was an **atheist**, meaning I didn't believe there was anything in the universe that cared whether I lived or died, or whether anybody else lived or died, and of course that didn't help. As an atheist I was sure **nothing** had a purpose. Nothing had meaning to me. I believed everything happened by chance, like a dice game. That was before I heard of **Einstein** and the famous words he said. Einstein said "God doesn't play dice with us," or something close to that. I don't think I could have discovered my life mission if I hadn't first given up being an atheist. Finally I did. Then I discovered my purpose. I discovered my mission and wrote it down. Then things started making sense. Then I could make sense even out of the pain.*

Floyd

as an anchor in the bottom of your boat, your life mission statement can be used to pull yourself out of the anger process when everything else fails. Your boat will reach shore no matter how far you are from the riverbank.

The Story of Viktor Frankl

The story of Viktor Frankl is often used to illustrate the power of having conscious awareness of your life mission. Viktor Frankl was a Jewish psychiatrist who spent four years in one of Adolph Hitler's Nazi concentration camps during World War II. Conditions in the camp were horrible. The conditions in the camp were so horrible, in fact, that they were almost beyond the comprehension of anyone who hadn't actually lived in one of the camps. The ratio of survival in the camp was 1 in 20. In other words, for every person who survived, 19 others died.

The Nazis did everything they could to strip away Frankl's humanity. They starved him. They beat him. They humiliated him unmercifully. But the Nazis could not break this courageous man, no matter what they did to him.

Allied soldiers liberated Frankl's camp at the end of the war. When they saw how bad things were in the camp, they were amazed to find Frankl and a few other prisoners still alive. The soldiers looked at the conditions of the camp. They saw the pathetic condition of the few survivors and could not believe their eyes. The emaciated bodies of the dead lay in heaps everywhere around them.

When the soldiers interviewed Frankl, they saw that Frankl had been treated no better than those in the camp who had died. The soldiers asked him how he managed to survive while so many others didn't. Here is what Viktor Frankl said:

"I survived because I had a mission."

At first the soldiers did not understand. They asked for clarification. Frankl said:

"I survived because I had a mission. My mission was, first, just to survive this camp; then to tell the whole world what happened here, so that no one would ever have to go through anything like this again."

That was Frankl's personal mission statement. That is what kept Frankl alive.

Frankl said he stayed focused on his mission. He said his mission made it possible to make sense out of what was happening to him. It made it possible for Frankl to make sense even out of the pain he had suffered at the hands of the concentration camp guards.

Frankl said he used his mission statement to manage his feelings. He used it to fight against fear and despair. *He used his mission to control the anger and rage he felt at the hands of the Nazis.* He said he knew he couldn't do or say anything in anger to his captors. They would kill him if he did.

Frankl said most of the prisoners who died didn't have a mission. Like Frankl, they had been beaten and starved, humiliated, and threatened. But unlike Frankl, they couldn't make sense out of the pain. Unable to make sense of the pain they were experiencing every minute of every day, they just could not endure. Some of them did or said angry things to the Nazis, and the Nazis killed them—murdered them, men, women, and children. Hitler's soldiers didn't care. Other prisoners became so despondent, so depressed, so empty, they simply lost all hope. They just gave up and died. Many committed suicide.

After his release from the concentration camp, Viktor Frankl went on to develop a new form of therapy. He called it Logo Therapy. In Greek, *logo* means "meaning." As a result of his concentration camp experiences, Frankl came to believe that people suffering from emotional or addictive disorders can experience spontaneous healing if they became consciously aware of their life mission. Frankl knew that people who have a conscious sense of purpose or mission can endure pain and discomfort well beyond anyone's expectations. He discovered that these people can live longer, happier lives than those who lack a sense of personal mission.

How To Discover Your Life Mission

Frankl did not know what his mission was before he went to the concentration camp. He may not even have known he had a mission. At first he couldn't make sense out of the pain he experienced in the camp any more than the other prisoners could. As conditions at the camp got worse, Frankl's condition got worse. His body and mind began to break down. Like the other prisoners, he, too, began to lose hope. Then out of deep despair, out of almost unendurable physical and emotional pain, Frankl asked himself a simple question: *"What is the meaning of my life? What is my special mission?"* The answer was, *"My mission is to survive this camp and then to tell the whole world what happened here, so that no other human being will ever have to go through anything like this again."*

In order to discover your life mission, you need to ask the same question Frankl asked: "What is the meaning of my life?" The answer to that question will be your life mission. But once you discover what your mission is, then you need to put the answer into words and write it down.

Why Should You Write Down Your Mission Statement?

You read Viktor Frankl's story above. You saw how he used his mission statement as a way to manage his feelings. You saw that he was able to use his mission statement to manage his anger. Frankl focused his attention on his mission for much of the time every day of his life in the camp. He was always aware of his mission, could always remember it. He kept it always in his consciousness, so that he would not forget it. Frankl knew that if he lost sight of his life mission, he would lose the will to live.

The reason you need to write down your mission is so that you will remember it. You will forget it if you don't write it down. If you forget your life mission, you will be unable to use it to help yourself make sense out of what is happening in your life.

Writing Your Mission Statement

Here are the ground rules:

1. Begin with your commitment to remain free from violence.

2. Your mission statement should be brief—25 words or less.

3. Your mission statement should cause you to have strong positive feelings about yourself, other people, and the world.

4. Your mission statement should reflect your highest values.

5. Your mission statement must benefit other people as well as yourself.

6. Your mission statement should make you feel a sense of urgency. Reading it should make you feel that you must fulfill your mission.

Here are some examples of life mission statements of some of the teens who wrote messages in some of the chapters of this guidebook.

John: "My life mission is to continue to recover from my anger habit, and help other teens stop their angry behavior."

Raymond: "This is my sacred path: to walk always in peace, and to help others see why we should never do anything to our Earth Mother without looking ahead seven generations to see what harm we might bring."

Raol: "My life mission is to be nonviolent while helping other teens learn how to feel safe without belonging to a gang."

MESSAGE FROM SEAN

Hi everybody. It's Sean again. Don't think this part of your recovery from your anger problem isn't important. I personally think it's the most important part of all. You can already tell it's not going to be easy to discover your mission and then put it down in words on paper. It was hard for me, and I call myself a writer. But I'm here to tell you that you can do it. It took me three tries. The first one was too long, and I left out some important stuff too. The second try got me closer. I got all the right stuff in the statement and in the right words, but it was too long, about forty words. I couldn't remember it all. Finally, I got it right. I made copies, as is suggested. I carried a copy around with me, lost it, dug out another copy, lost that one. Finally, I read it over enough times so that it stuck. Then I bought an MP3 player. I recorded my mission statement on my computer, then downloaded it on my player. I listened to it every day, and still do. I'm glad, too, because the recording I downloaded saved me from going over the Falls one time. I'll tell you about that later. Anyway, now it doesn't matter what's going on around me, I can remember it word for word, even when I'm in the river and getting close to the Falls. I still say it to myself in the morning and again at night before I go to sleep. It's saved my butt more than once. Still, I think it might be time to take another look, and tweak it some more.

Sean

Once you have completed your mission statement, make several copies. Keep a copy of your mission statement in your pocket or purse. Tape a copy to the wall next to your bed. Read your mission statement at least once in the morning and once at night before going to sleep. Read it every time an anger trigger occurs. If possible, record your mission statement on a CD, iPod, or MP3. Listen to the recording one or more times a day.

Write your mission statement on the following page. Use a pencil, so you can erase as you go along. Take your time. This is a very important part of the healing process, so take it seriously. You will have to write more than one draft. You may need to write three or more drafts before your mission statement is really complete. If you think you are done after just one or two attempts, review it to make sure you are satisfied.

My life mission is to remain violence-free and . . .

_____

_____

_____

_____

_____

_____

_____

_____

_____

_____

_____

_____

_____

_____

_____

_____

_____

_____

_____

_____

_____

_____

Mission Support

You have discovered your mission and have written it down. Now you need to stop and think about mission support. Every mission requires support. Mountain climbers don't start off on a mission to conquer a 20,000-foot mountain without mission support. They need supplies to accomplish their mission. Astronauts don't start on a mission without a lot of support. They need food, water, oxygen, and many other things to support them on their mission. Your mission needs support too. Your mission support consists of feelings—positive feelings. In order to succeed on your mission, you must maintain a positive emotional state as much of the time as possible. You need to feel good feelings, consistently. Of course you can't feel good all of the time, but in order to stay on your mission you need to feel good most of the time. Positive feelings help you stay on course. They help you keep moving in the right direction. Negative feelings will send you off course, away from your mission. Anger is a negative feeling, so anger will knock you off course. Confidence is a positive feeling. Confidence will keep you on course.

You need to make a list of the positive feelings that represent your mission support. You may refer back to Chapter 15 where you listed your valued feelings. Your valued feelings are the kind of positive feelings you will need to include on your mission support list. If you did a thorough job of writing your valued feelings list, you can use the valued feelings you wrote down to get started on your mission support list. Write your positive feelings on the form provided below. Try to list at least 25 positive feelings on your mission support list.

Mission Support List

_____

_____

_____

_____

_____

_____

_____

_____

_____

_____

_____

_____

_____

_____

_____

_____

_____

_____

_____

_____

_____

_____

_____

_____

MESSAGE FROM SEAN

When I discovered my mission, things happened that made me real aware of its power. I mentioned some of the things in my story in Chapter 1. So excuse me for repeating myself. One of the things that happened, was I was walking down the hall at my high school my last year there, when somebody bumped into me. I'm not sure if he bumped into me or I bumped into him. I was thinking about something and was looking up at the ceiling instead of watching where I was going. Anyhow, this other person and I collided. My book bag was in my locker, so I was carrying books under my arm. They went all over the floor. I had my MP3 player hooked on my belt. Somehow it got loose and went skidding across the floor too. The dude I bumped into, another senior, saw my MP3 player on the floor. He went over and deliberately stepped on it. Right away tunes started to play. The dude gave my MP3 player a kick and sent it skidding again. Somehow, the player skipped forward a couple of tracks, the music stopped, and some words started to play. Try and guess what they were. C'mon, try! Give up? Okay, the kick the dude gave my MP3 player made it jump to where I'd recorded my mission statement! Can you believe it? I mean, I'd already dropped into my attack posture that I'd been trained to do in karate class for almost ten years. I was about to lay a kick on the dude that could've sent him to the hospital. The adrenaline was pumping a thousand miles an hour. I was drilling the dude with my eyes, my brain was measuring distance from me to him, and my foot was off the floor aimed right at the dude—right at you-know-where. My tension level was peaked. I mean I was in white water, man. Meanwhile, my mission statement was playing somewhere down on the floor loud enough for me to hear. Somehow, the words penetrated through my rage. So there I was ready to attack. The dude was in my karate class but only had a couple of years experience. He was standing frozen in his tracks, the blood all drained out of his face. He'd seen me work out before in karate school, knew I'd been studying for 'bout ten years. And he knew he was about to get hurt real bad, maybe crippled. I was ready to do it, couldn't wait to hurt him. I was in full tilt automatic karate attack mode, and—that's when it happened. The words coming out of my MP3 player somehow got through to me. The kick I'd started to throw stopped in mid-air, like some giant immovable hand had suddenly grabbed my foot. I'd rather not tell this next part, b'cuz it's kinda embarrassing. But Pathways to Peace is an honest program, right? So here goes. Stopping the kick made me lose my balance. I tried to catch myself in time, but couldn't. I'd never stopped a kick in mid-air like that before, so my brain didn't know exactly what to do. Yep, you guessed it. I ended up on my butt. Just before I got back on my feet, I glanced up at the dude's face. Fortunately for him and me, both, he didn't have a smile on his face. He still

> *looked pretty scared. The dude apologized all over the place. I said I was sorry too. I wasn't too sincere. But I was glad I hadn't let my anger override my mission; for that I was sincerely glad. Here's my mission. It's meant to be read to a rap beat:*
>
> > *My sacred life mission,*
> > *which gives meaning to my being,*
> > *is to use the spoken words I write*
> > *everywhere I go*
> > *to help every angry teen I meet*
> > *find what we all deserve and long for:*
> > *to walk content and unafraid*
> > *through this world of war and hate*
> > *along a pathway to peace.*
>
> *I know it's longer than the recommended 25 words. But I can get away with it, b'cuz I rap the words every day. I've even performed it a couple times at a local coffee house that lets teens come and do their thing on open-mike night. The words are burned into my brain like a CD.*
>
> *Sean*

Spirituality

You have a spiritual part, whether you know it or not. All people have a spiritual part. In Chapter 6, the spiritual part was defined as that part of your whole self which helps you to feel connected. The spiritual part helps you feel connected in a positive way to other people. It helps you feel connected to the rest of the universe. It helps you feel connected to the higher power of your understanding. That is what is meant by the word "spiritual." Used in this way, in this book, it does not mean religion. Religion is the way people choose to express their spiritual side. Perhaps you were raised in one of the major religions of the world, such as Hinduism, Buddhism, Taoism, Judaism, Islam, or Christianity. Maybe you were raised in one of the lesser known religions, such as Shintoism or Spiritism. Maybe you are a Native American and were raised in the Long House Religion. Maybe you are an agnostic (one who isn't sure of the existence of a higher power) or an atheist (one who is certain no such thing exists), in which case you may not believe in any recognized religion. Whatever your religious orientation may or may not be, it is your business. The message here is this, and only this: *All human beings appear to have a part of their whole self that can be called the spiritual part.*

As was also pointed out earlier in the guidebook, if you feel spiritually connected, you may end up discovering a purpose which is even bigger than your personal mission. Whatever the case may be, to recover fully requires paying some attention to your spiritual part. If you have not yet begun to explore your spiritual part, it is strongly suggested that you begin your spiritual exploration now.

MESSAGE FROM SEAN

Hi. This is Sean. Glad I have a chance to talk about this subject. The whole thing on spirituality—I didn't want to hear about it. My mom was raised Catholic. She had bad experiences at parochial school. The nuns weren't too kind, she said. One of the priests sexually abused her brother. I know that happens sometimes in Protestant churches too, and in public schools. But my mom was really down on religion. Not just down on the Catholic religion, she was down on all religions. She told me they were all just a big scam. I grew up thinking the same thing. I became an atheist. That's some-body who doesn't believe there's anything bigger than himself. Pretty ego-tistical, right? But my Pathways to Peace sponsor finally talked me into pay-ing some attention to that part of my whole self. I did some reading. Asked some questions. I found out spirituality didn't necessarily mean religion. Fi-nally, I adopted the Pathways to Peace idea that spirituality means feeling connected to other people, to the rest of the world, and to something big-ger than myself—something higher. I also learned that feeling connected in a spiritual way could help me make sense out of things when they didn't make sense any other way. I read about different religions. I mean all the main ones. None of them turned me on. So I gave up. But that didn't work either, because now I knew enough about the spiritual part of my self to know I couldn't just ignore it. Not having something higher than myself to believe in made me feel—well, like I wasn't a complete person. Like some-thing real important was missing. I couldn't just grab onto anything just to have something to grab onto.

*I gave spirituality a lot of thought. Then one day when I was writing in my journal, it came to me. Sometimes when I'm writing a rap, it seems like the words don't come from me at all. Sometimes it feels like the words just sort of flow through me. At those times it's like I'm some kind of a hollow tube, like the barrel of my pen. I remembered reading about other writers who felt that way too, once in a while. One of them, a Beat poet from the 1950s, said when he felt that way it was because the Muse was working through him. So after a while, I got to thinking that maybe that's where the words came from when I felt that way—from the Muse. Maybe the Muse worked through me sometimes. The word **muse** comes from Greek mythology. It's the power behind poetry, painting, music, and the other arts. The ancient Greeks thought the Muse was a goddess who lived on Olympus with her sisters.*

*Anyhow, I still don't know about **God**. But I believe in the Muse. Maybe some day I'll go after spirituality in a bigger way, but right now the Muse will do. I call her **The Lady**, the one who gives me words and moves my hand when I sit down to write a poem or compose a rap.*

Sean

MESSAGE FROM RAYMOND

Hi. It's me, the Seneca guy. Remember? I was pretty confused by the spiritual part. I grew up on the Rez. I went to a couple different churches, both of them Christian churches. There's another church on the Rez, a real small one with only about 40 members. It's where the Long House Religion has its services. The Long House Religion mixes Christianity in with old-time Iroquois beliefs. When I got sober, I started going there with my uncle. That's one of the rules of the Long House Religion—you have to be a sober Indian to go there. It's my religion. It's how I choose to express my spiritual part—hey, it's what I believe!

I learned a prayer from one of the Long House elders. They say a Lakota Indian man wrote it way back about 1890. But now all the Indian tribes know that prayer, because it speaks to us Indians in a special way. The prayer is called "Let Me Walk in Beauty."

Great Mystery whose voice I hear on the winds, and whose breath gives life to all the world, hear me. I stand before you, one of your many children.

Small and weak, I need your strength and wisdom. Let me walk in beauty, and make my eyes ever behold the red and purple sunset.

Make my hands respect the things you have made, my ears sharp to hear your voice. Make me wise, that I might know the things you have taught my people, the lessons you have hidden in every leaf and rock.

Great Mystery, I seek strength not to be superior to my brothers and sisters, but to be able to fight my greatest enemy—myself.

Great Mystery, make me always ready to come to you with clean hands and straight eyes, so when life fades as a fading sunset, my spirit may come to you without shame.

That's my prayer and what I try to live by. It's my mission too, so every time I think of this prayer I think of my mission.

Raymond

CHAPTER SEVENTEEN

Establish Meaningful Goals

You have a mission. Now you need *meaningful goals*. A goal is meaningful when it reflects one or more of your highest values and when it helps you move along on your mission. In fact, one of the main purposes of a goal is to let you know that you are moving along on your mission. Goals, which are closely connected to values, also help you stay focused on your mission. Your main goal, of course, needs to be to maintain your behavior change. Maintaining your new violence-free lifestyle needs to continue to be your most important goal. You have many good reasons to maintain that goal. To keep your freedom. To maintain your self-respect. To fulfill your special purpose.

A goal is always based on *needs* or *wants*. Goals are things you need or things that you desire to have. Merely needing something or desiring something won't make what you need or desire come into your life. You may need a new pair of shoes, and you have a strong desire to obtain them. But until you focus on a new pair of shoes as a goal, and put a plan of action in place, you will never obtain a new pair of shoes. You will sit in your chair needing a new pair of shoes, and the shoes will sit on the shelf at the shoe store needing a buyer. But nothing will ever come of it. Changing your angry behavior has to be a goal, not just a need. Otherwise, nothing will come of that either.

You have decided not to use anger to feel important and powerful and, instead, to work an anger management program to avoid falling back into angry behavior.

Staying violence-free must always be your number one goal. That is your big goal. But now you need to set other goals, too. You need to set goals around each of the Eight Steps of Recovery, because, as you have learned, full recovery requires you to strive for balance in your life around all eight parts of your whole self. The goals you set in each of the Eight Steps of Recovery will take you to your main goal.

What is a Goal?

You already know what a goal is not. A goal is not a wish or a dream. Wishes and dreams are vague ideas about the future. A goal is a clearly defined, reachable, future destination. It is the end of a carefully designed plan.

Goals Have Six Elements

As we are using the word "goal" in this chapter, a goal:

1. Must be a clear statement about something you really want.
2. Must be positive and move you forward in your recovery and toward your mission.
3. Must be reachable and clearly specified in writing.
4. Must include a time frame.
5. Must include a method that has immediate action steps.
6. Must include a way to measure progress.

If a goal does not include these six elements, it is not a goal. It is a wish or a dream.

Steps to Successful Goal Setting and Goal Achievement

Goal setting and goal achievement are a four-step process. You need to make four decisions and then follow through on your decisions.

Step One: *Defining or Choosing the Goal*

First, you need to decide on a reachable goal. Ask yourself if the goal you want to set is reachable. If in doubt, ask others for their opinion. You must be specific. Ask yourself *exactly* what you want to accomplish. Let's say you decide you want to lose weight. Saying that your goal is simply to lose weight is not specific enough. You must specify the amount of weight you want to lose. Let's say you decide to lose ten pounds. Ten pounds is specific.

Step Two: *Setting the Time Frame*

Now you need to decide exactly *when* you want to lose the ten pounds. Let's say you decide on a month-long time frame. Let's assume that today is the first day of January. If today is the first of January, then the first of February would be your target date, exactly a month from today.

Step Three: *Planning the Method and Taking Action*

Next, you must decide on a method and then take immediate action. Let's say you decide to:

A. Reduce your intake of carbohydrates to below 120 grams per day, and increase your intake of protein to 100 grams per day (the figures given are used only as examples and meant only to illustrate this part of the goal setting and goal achievement method).

B. Exercise three times each week for 45 minutes.

C. Take these action steps:

    1. Go to the store and buy a carbohydrate/protein gram counter.

    2. Use the carbohydrate/protein gram counter as a guide for meal preparation.

    3. Join a health club and take your first workout.

Step Four: *Keeping Track of Your Progress*

Now you must decide how to measure your progress. If you don't know whether or not you are moving toward your goal, you will lose interest. Then you will give up and you will not achieve your goal.

You need to consider the best way to measure the progress you are making toward your goal. If you wear a belt, you could check your belt notches. That's one way to see if you are losing weight and moving toward your goal. But you could lose inches by exercising and still not lose weight. So that may not be a good way to measure your progress. You could weigh yourself the day you start your program, then weigh yourself once a week and see exactly how many pounds you have lost. A scale would give you an accurate way of measuring your progress. There would be no guess work.

Now you can write a clear, specific goal statement which would look and sound like this:

> *I will lose 10 pounds by the first of February, one month from today. I will reduce my intake of carbohydrates to below 100 grams per day and increase*

my protein to 100 grams. I will exercise 45 minutes three times a week. I will weigh myself once a week to check my progress.

Now you have a clearly defined destination. You have a plan, and you have taken action. You have a real goal, not just a vague wish or dream for the future. Here is an outline of the steps:

1. Decide on a specific **goal** and write it down.
2. Decide on a specific **time** frame.
3. Decide on a **method** and take immediate action.
4. Decide on a way to **measure** your progress.

You can apply this goal setting and goal achievement formula to any goal. If the goal is reachable you will succeed.

. . . .

SELF-TEST

1. One of the main purposes of a goal is to let you know that you are moving along on your mission.

    TRUE   FALSE

2. Your main goal needs to be to maintain your behavior change.

    TRUE   FALSE

3. The goals you set in each of the Eight Steps of Recovery will take you to your main goal.

    TRUE   FALSE

4. What exactly is a goal?

5. Write down the six elements of a goal.

1. _____
2. _____
3. _____
4. _____
5. _____
6. _____

6. Write down the four steps to successful goal setting and goal achievement.

1. _____
2. _____
3. _____
4. _____

. . . .

Recovery Goals and the Eight Parts of the Whole Self

Start by thinking about the Eight Parts of the Whole Self, which we discussed in Chapter 6. The Eight Parts of the Whole Self provide the framework for setting your recovery goals. Your goals should lead to improvement in each part. Let's review these parts as goals:

1. **Biological (physical) Goals**: goals for the health of your body.

2. **Environment Goals**: goals about where you will live and whom you will spend time with.

3. **Behavior Goals**: goals about your actions and words.

4. **Skill Goals**: goals about learning new things and acquiring new tools.

5. **Value Goals**: goals about expanding your values.

6. **Belief Goals**: goals about letting go of limiting beliefs and adopting new beliefs that support your recovery.

7. **Mission Goals**: goals that move you toward your mission.

8. **Spiritual Goals**: goals that help you feel connected in a positive way to others, to the world, and to the higher power of your understanding.

Take a minute and consider Part One of the Whole Self, the biological (physical) self. Ask yourself, "What must I do to improve the biological (physical) part of my self?" Using the word "must" instead of "could" makes it more likely you will follow through. Then list one or two things you must do to improve that part of your self.

Then go on to the next part. Ask yourself, "What must I do to improve the environmental part of my self?" Then write down one or two things you must do to improve that part.

Follow this procedure for each of the Eight Parts of the Whole Self. Two examples are given below for each part, to help you get you started. Your job is to come up with one to three more goals for each part of your whole self.

It is important to understand the nature of goals and the power they have in your life. Goals are what you want to move toward that will lead to the feelings you want and deserve. Goals help you satisfy your positive values. You want to stay happily free of excessive anger, so you need to be goal-oriented. Remember: goals keep you on track and move you toward your mission.

Biological Goals:

1. Stop smoking by my next birthday.
2. Attain my ideal weight by June 1st.
3. _____
4. _____
5. _____

Environment Goals:

1. Listen to relaxing music 15 minutes a day over the next three months.
2. Make two new non-violent friends within two weeks from this date.
3. _____

4. _____

5. _____

Behavior Goals:

1. Notice when I am speaking too loudly and immediately reduce the volume of my voice.

2. Become aware when I'm breathing too rapidly due to stress, and slow down my breathing.

3. _____

4. _____

5. _____

Skills Goals:

1. Learn how to relax, when feeling stressed, in less than two minutes.

2. Teach relaxation skills to one other person within 30 days.

3. _____

4. _____

5. _____

Values Goals:

1. Read my values list every morning before I leave the house.

2. Discover two more of my valued feelings within two weeks.

3. _____

4. _____

5. _____

Beliefs Goals:

1. Identify two more of my negative beliefs and change them within 30 days.

2. Adopt two positive beliefs about other people by the end of this month.

3. _____

4. _____

5. _____

Mission Goals:

1. Memorize my mission statement within one week.

2. Recite my mission statement once at night and once in the morning, starting tonight.

3. _____

4. _____

5. _____

Spiritual Goals:

1. Read from spiritual literature at least once a day, starting today.

2. Visit two different churches or places of worship within the next 30 days.

3. _____

4. _____

5. _____

Moving Toward Your Goals

In the past you were motivated to use anger and rage in order to move away from painful feelings, such as anxiety or frustration, embarrassment or fear. As you continue your recovery from your anger habit, you will sometimes find yourself without resources to move away from painful things and conditions. Goals will help you move toward positive feelings and things. The reason you decided to change your behavior in the first place may have been to avoid further pain of negative results. Now you will have positive goals to move toward that will help you feel better about yourself and the world.

You need to learn to focus more time and energy on your goals. Achieving goals will help you go beyond the mere avoidance of the painful results you know you will suffer if you relapse back into your old angry behavior. Your goals will help you find the kind of fulfilled and happy life that you deserve.

As soon as you set a goal, things start happening. Your brain automatically gathers its resources to get you to your goal. Your brain will take you anywhere you want, but you have to tell it exactly where you want to go. You need to put it in writing.

Goals will keep you moving toward your mission. Your mission will let you know that recovery is more than the mere absence of violence, more than the absence of pain.

Setting a Goal to Stop Using Anger and Violence

You want to stop using anger and violence to *change* how you feel, and you want to stay stopped. Therefore, as you have learned, you need to make it a goal. And you need to write it down. Your goal statement must include the benefits of stopping, as well as the negative results of continuing the behavior. When writing your goal, use language that makes you feel you have no choice but to stop using anger and rage immediately. Follow the instructions below:

1. Write down a clear, concise goal statement (less than 20 words), including the time frame. Example: "I will stop using anger and violence to feel powerful over people, places, and things, beginning this date: _____."

2. Write down three specific benefits you believe would make the effort worthwhile. Examples: "Fewer restrictions and more freedom in my personal life. Improved relationship with my parents. More choices, and able to make more of my own decisions."

Benefits:

1. _____

2. _____

3. _____

3. Write down three specific losses that you know would cause you severe emotional pain if you don't stop using anger to *change* how you feel. Examples: "I will get expelled from high school. I will lose my present relationship or miss out on developing a relationship with someone I really like. I might get into serious trouble and get sent to the Detention Center (again)."

Losses:

1. _____

2. _____

3. _____

4. Look at the losses you listed. Now close your eyes and visualize experiencing the losses. Allow yourself to get in touch with the pain those losses will cause. Example: imagine yourself in the Detention Center, separated from your friends and loved ones, with nothing to do except think about your loss of freedom. Spend one or two minutes doing this step.

5. Look at the benefits list, then close your eyes and visualize experiencing the benefits. See an image of yourself responding differently to old anger triggers and enjoying each of the benefits. Spend three to five minutes doing this step.

6. Review Step 4 once daily in the morning. Then review Step 5. Repeat Steps 4 and 5 again in the evening before going to sleep.

All the goals you set should fit into, and move you toward, your mission. They are an important part of your mission support.

CHAPTER EIGHTEEN

Forgiveness

The Importance of Forgiveness

Forgiveness is the final step in the recovery process. It is part of the Eighth Principle. The word "forgive" means to cease to resent. It means to pardon or release.

Like Sean and some of the other teens who shared parts of their stories in this workbook, you may have had awful things done to you in the past. Some of the things you have done to others may have been as awful as what was done to you. But, in order to heal from your anger habit, you need to forgive those who harmed you, and you need to forgive yourself. You need to cease to resent those who harmed you, and you need to pardon and release yourself from guilt and shame.

Unless you forgive others, the feelings of humiliation and resentment that have kept you stuck in anger and rage will continue. Unless you forgive yourself, your feelings of guilt and shame will keep you trapped in angry behavior. For you, these negative feelings are triggers for anger and rage. They will rise up from the past like ghosts, to trigger your anger. They will plunge you into the river and you will end up going over the Falls.

Forgiving others will release you from the deep resentment that keeps you stuck in anger. Forgiving yourself will release you from toxic guilt and shame. Unless you forgive, the memories of what was done to you and what you have done to others will continue to haunt you.

Once you forgive, you will be amazed. You will know how the caged bird feels when it is released and why it sings. You will move with enormous energy toward your goals. You will discover the joy that can be found in service to others. You will make a giant leap toward your mission. You will know the meaning of serenity. You will feel connected to others, to the world, and to the God of your understanding as never before. You will feel transformed.

But forgiving is not an easy thing to do. The hardest part of forgiveness is getting past negative beliefs that you might hold about forgiveness. Look at the examples of negative beliefs about forgiveness listed below:

Forgiveness will encourage people to take advantage of me.

I could never forgive those who caused me so much pain.

Those who hurt me don't deserve to be forgiven.

I don't deserve to be forgiven.

I can't forgive myself.

. . . .

SELF-TEST

1.   Forgiveness is the final step in the recovery process.

TRUE   FALSE

2.   Forgiving yourself and others releases you from resentment and from toxic guilt and shame.

TRUE   FALSE

3.   Write down in a few words what the word "forgiveness" means.

. . . .

Forgiving Others

In order to change your angry behavior and recover from your anger habit, you need to forgive those who harmed you in the past—no matter how much you may have suffered as a result of what was done to you. No matter how great the pain, no matter how deep the scars on your body or in your mind, you need to find it in your heart to forgive those who harmed you. You cannot afford to hold on to your resentment and hate. If you refuse to forgive, eventually you will fall back into your old angry behaviors. You cannot heal unless you forgive. Unless you forgive, you will never be happy. These are strong words, there is no denying that. But they are true.

In order to forgive, you do not have to forget. In fact it is not even possible to forget. You can repress the memories. But, as you have already learned, you cannot forget what has been done to you. You can stop the memories of what was done to you from intruding so much, and so much of the time, in the here and now by using the skills you learned. But you cannot, and will not, forget those memories.

When you forgive, you will stop thinking so much and so often about those who harmed you. You will stop thinking about what they did. Once you forgive, your overall tension level will decrease and you will feel less anxiety as you go about your daily life. You will have fewer anger outbursts. You will have more positive energy to deal with stressful things that occur every day in the here and now.

As you forgive all those who have harmed you, remember this: You are not forgiving them for their good. You are forgiving them for *your own good*.

. . . .

SELF-TEST

1. Make a list of people who have harmed you the most, and toward whom you have very strong feelings of anger. Briefly state what each person did to you and how it made you feel.

   Example:

   Name: My father.
   What the person did: He came home drunk and beat me up.
   How it made me feel: I felt scared and unloved.

   Name: _____

   What the person did: _____

   How it made me feel: _____

   Name: _____

   What the person did: _____

   How it made me feel: _____

Name: _____

What the person did: _____

How it made me feel: _____

Name: _____

What the person did: _____

How it made me feel: _____

Name: _____

What the person did: _____

How it made me feel: _____

2. Find a quiet place to sit. Read the statement below to yourself, filling in the blank with the name of the person you have decided to forgive. Use a pencil, instead of a pen. There may be more than one person you need to forgive, but start with one person. When you feel you have really forgiven that person, erase the first name and write the next person's name in the blank.

> *I forgive you, _____, not because I have forgotten, or gotten over, what you did to me. I forgive you not just because I want to be free of the pain you inflicted on me. I forgive you so that I may be free of the anger it has caused in my life, and which contributed to the pain I have caused others. I forgive you so that I may break the cycle of anger and hate and violence. I forgive you so that I may never again use what you did to me as an excuse to hurt others.*

After you have completed the exercise, tell your counselor or call your Pathways to Peace sponsor or a Pathways to Peace friend, and tell them what you have just accomplished. Share it in a general way, but not in detail and without mentioning names, at your next Pathways to Peace meeting. Open yourself up to feedback from the group. Enjoy the warmth of the good things people will say to you, because they will understand how hard it is to apply that part of the Eighth Principle of Pathways to Peace.

You may need to repeat this exercise more than once. You may need to repeat it many times before you feel you have truly forgiven those who harmed you. Repeat the exercise once or twice a day, until you really feel you have forgiven.

. . . .

Forgiving Yourself

You also need to forgive yourself. Failing to take whatever steps may be required to accomplish self-forgiveness would stop you short of your main goal. It would be like climbing the mountain, only to stop and hide in the shadows of a cave just a few yards from the summit and deprive yourself of the spectacular view that would be your reward. You have come this far. You have struggled as few human beings have struggled. You deserve to win the prize. So don't stop now. Go all the way to the mountain top.

As in the exercise on forgiving others, find a quiet place to sit alone. Read the statement below to yourself. When you have finished, share what you have accomplished with another person. Share it with your counselor or with your Pathways to Peace sponsor, or with a Pathways to Peace friend.

1. Make a list of people you have harmed because of your anger. Next to each name, briefly state what you did or what you said to the person. You can refer back to the list you made of people you have harmed, and include those names on your list. If you feel you have done major harm to more than five people, you can add them on a separate sheet of paper.

   Example:
   Name: John (my little brother)
   What I did: I screamed at John and called him stupid.
   The result: John broke down and cried.

   Name: _____

   What I did: _____

   The result: _____

Name: _____

What I did: _____

The result: _____

Name: _____

What I did: _____

The result: _____

2. Find a quiet place to sit, then read the statement below to yourself.

    > *I forgive myself for hurting _____, not because I feel what I did is excusable in any way, or that I do not deserve the consequences I suffered for what I did, or may suffer in the future, because of my actions. I forgive myself so that I may heal from the overwhelming guilt I have felt, and which would continue to trigger my anger and rage, in the future, against others as well as myself.*

    Repeat this exercise at least once a day until you really feel you have forgiven yourself.

Forgiveness is an ongoing process. Be patient with yourself. If the anger and hurt keep coming back, you know you are not finished. Work at it. You'll know when you are done—the pain will go away.

Review and Follow-Up

Early in the guidebook, you were asked to become willing to forgive. You did some exercises about making amends to people you had hurt. Review the work you did. Do you need to follow up your forgiveness exercise with some more amends work? If so, now is the time.

MESSAGE FROM GREG

I haven't forgiven everybody yet, and haven't forgiven myself either for some of the things I did. But one of the people I did forgive was somebody I never thought I could. It happened a couple of years ago. I was out walking late one night after a party, drunk, and I ended up in a part of the city we call the white ghetto. The people who live there are poor, their neighborhood is run down like mine. There's some pretty tough gangs there too. Anyway, it was the wrong neighborhood for a black guy to end up in. I got beat up real bad that night. I knew the guy who did it. We both went to the same old broken down ghetto school. He had two other white guys hold me.

Man, I had a resentment for that white boy that wouldn't quit. I used to dream about what I'd do to him if I ever saw him on my turf. Not long after I got in Pathways to Peace, the guy that beat me up got killed in a car wreck. He died, but my resentment didn't. Every time I thought about him, I got angry all over again. It seemed like his ghost was determined to keep on being a trigger for my anger. Then one night I sat down and wrote a rap. It's kinda based on a poem by some old English poet from the 1600s that I was forced to read last year when I was in 10th grade. Actually, that old poet said some interesting things. His name was John Donne. The poem was about how death doesn't have any boundaries. There's no South Side or East Side, and nobody gets left out, and nobody's more important than somebody else, and we're all related no matter what color we are or what we believe in or where we lived when we were alive. The poem ends with a church bell ringing to let everybody know somebody died. Anyway I wrote this rap based on that old poem, with the guy from the white ghetto who died in the car wreck in mind. It worked. The rap I wrote made me forgive him. Here it is.

Death Rap

Black or white, man or woman—it don't matter what we look like.
Greedy rich respectable, ghetto poor forgotten—
it don't matter who we are.
East Side or South Town, Uptown or Down—
it don't matter where we find ourselves, it don't matter where we live.
B'cuz we're all a part of man and womankind—
it's all we need to know
in order to forgive.

Greg

My name is Anne. I'm eighteen. I live in San Diego and I used to use anger like a drug. I know how important forgiveness is. I was seventeen before I began my recovery. I was full of rage. My stepfather had abused me…if you know what I mean. I was in sixth grade when he did it the first time. My mother found out when I was thirteen. She wanted to kill him. Instead she took me away. I was angry at my stepfather for what he did. I was angry at my mother for taking me away. I was so confused! And I took my anger out on everybody. I paid some dues, I want you to know. Got expelled from school, went to the Detention Center—you know what I mean by dues. Finally, I saw I had a bad problem with anger. I got some help from a counselor. I changed some of my behavior real fast. But I wanted to be happy, not just non-violent, so I knew I had to forgive. I forgave my stepfather in an unsent letter. I had to write that letter twenty times! I forgave my mother face-to-face. Finally, I forgave myself. Believe it or not, forgiving myself was the hardest part. Having forgiven others as well as myself, I started growing fast—I mean fast! Sometimes it feels like my life is still a mess, but there are times when it feels wonderful! Most of the time, now, I feel good about myself, and most of the time I feel good about other people. That's totally different than it used to be.

Anne

Self-Contract

When you began this book you signed a 14-point self-agreement. You have now completed the book. Completing this book was a major task, so you should be proud of yourself. It is a great beginning! Now you need to continue to apply what you have learned.

Now it is time to sign a self-contract. A self-contract is stronger than an agreement. An agreement indicates you will try to fulfill the points of the agreement to the best of your ability at the time it was written. A contract is a promise—a total commitment. A self-contract means you are committed to the task of someday fulfilling all the points of the contract. Period.

Now you understand anger and rage, and you know how to change your angry behavior and stop the violence. Now there are no excuses. Now you are ready for a self-contract.

Look at the self-contract on the next page. Do not enter into it lightly. If you violate your self-contract, you violate yourself, no one else.

You will want to have someone you like and admire witness your signature.

I, _____, am now totally committed to living a violence-free life as of this date,_____, and will continue to live by the following principles from this day on.

1. I have admitted I have a problem with anger and have harmed others, property, and myself. I have apologized and made restitution wherever possible.

2. I now accept personal responsibility for the results of my actions, and have made a decision to stop my harmful behavior.

3. I once used threats and verbal or physical violence to feel powerful. I now understand that I was never justified in using violence, and never will be justified.

4. I have learned, and will continue to learn, new ways to feel personal power that do not violate other people's right to feel safe in their person and property.

5. I am totally committed to treating all people with respect and dignity.

6. I now believe I have the ability to change and grow.

7. I believe I have a purpose which goes beyond my own personal desires.

8. I have forgiven those who harmed me and have forgiven myself for the harm I have done others, and will continue to do so whenever necessary.

9. I am committed to helping others recover from anger, rage, and violence.

10. I am committed to continuing my path of emotional, mental, and spiritual growth.

11. I understand that violating this contract is a violation of myself.

Date: _____

Signature:_____

Witness:_____

Congratulations! You have just completed a major task. The book you have just finished required a lot of study and effort. But your job has just begun. Now you need to maintain the changes you have made, and you need to make yet more changes. You need to continue to grow and continue to work all of the Eight Steps of your recovery every day.

You may already be a member of Pathways to Peace. If not, you are strongly encouraged to join a Pathways to Peace group in your area as soon as possible. You may need the influence of a Pathways to Peace group to help you stay on track. You may need a Pathways to Peace sponsor to help you along.

MESSAGE FROM SEAN

I want to say congratulations, too! Like Bill, the guy who wrote the book, said, you've just finished a major task. I know it wasn't easy, because I did it too. Writing my story in the beginning of the book and then jumping in throughout the book with my messages was like doing the whole thing all over again. It was, in fact, b'cuz I had to read everything again too. And while I was at it, I decided I might as well do the self-tests again. I'm glad I did, b'cuz I learned some more stuff about anger and how to stay out of the river. And I learned more about myself too—a lot more. If I was to give you any advice, which I'd never do b'cuz I know you'd never listen, I'd say to wait a few weeks or a few months, or whatever feels right to you, and then go back and read the whole book again. And while you're at it, do the self-tests again too.

I don't know where you're at with your program, whether you've just started or have been around for a year or two. If you've read the book and have been working the Pathways to Peace program for at least a few months, then you've probably already gotten some benefits. You're probably doing better in school. Probably getting along better with your family too, or getting along better with whoever's helping you get what you need in order to get through your teen years okay. Maybe you've found out that things won't always go smooth. Right? You know that by now. Well, that's life. I mean, what can I say? But even when things feel like they're worse than ever, don't do anything to mess yourself up again! Believe me, if you go back to your old behavior, things won't be like they used to be. Nope, they'll be worse than ever. Worse than you can imagine.

Sean

MESSAGE FROM WALT

I know Sean. Met him at his first Pathways to Peace meeting. By the way, I'm writing this from prison. Are you impressed? Don't be. Don't think I'm some kind of cult hero because I'm locked up behind some thick gray walls. I'm sitting in this cramped little cell because I went back to my old angry ways. One night I got drunk and got in a fight with some dude at a party. He was drunk too, and was doing meth. He said something about me that made me feel embarrassed, and that triggered my anger. It was a bad fight. The dude had a knife. I tried to get it away from him. We wrestled around on the floor. All of a sudden, the dude got real quiet. I got up, but he didn't. If I'm real lucky, I might be out in ten more years.

Walt

APPENDIX A

The Pathways to Peace Self-Help Program

What is Pathways to Peace?

Pathways to Peace, Inc., is a self-help program for people who have problems with anger. Members meet in groups once a week or more, to help each other understand anger and rage and to help each other stop angry behavior. Group members help each other by sharing their stories and by showing each other they can change. There are Pathways to Peace groups in the United States and Canada, and membership continues to grow. Anyone with an anger problem may participate in a Pathways to Peace group. Having a problem with anger is the only requirement. While participation in a Pathways to Peace group is free, members are expected to purchase their own workbooks. Two workbooks are used, depending on age:

- *Pathways to Peace Anger Management Workbook* (for adults)
- *Managing Teen Anger and Violence* (for teens)

For your convenience, both books can be ordered from Impact Publications (see the order form at the back of this workbook).

The Pathways to Peace Purpose

The Pathways to Peace purpose is clear: Our purpose, or mission, is to help people stop physical and verbal violence; to help people discover and pursue their highest values; to help people reach their goals; to help people learn how to grow, to heal, and to help others who have a problem with anger.

Pathways to Peace Member Profile

Pathways to Peace members come from all walks of life, from all over the world. They are people of every race and religion and are of all ages, including adults and teens. Some are married, some are divorced or separated, some have never been married. Some are still in school and live at home with parents or guardians. Some Pathways to Peace members have been in prison because of anger. Some members are told they must attend Pathways to Peace; some are encouraged by others to attend. Some members attend Pathways to Peace on their own. They came to Pathways to Peace because they felt guilty or ashamed, or because they lost something they valued as a result of angry behavior. Some members lost their wives or husbands; some lost their children; some lost their jobs; some lost their freedom; some lost their educational opportunities. All Pathways to Peace members had problems due to anger. All had harmed others; all are trying to change; all are trying to put the past behind and create a better future for themselves.

The Pathways to Peace Principles

Principle One: *We admit we have a problem with anger and have harmed people, property, and ourselves. Whenever possible, we will make amends or restitution.*

This is the first step to recovery. We wanted to change our angry behavior and stop the violence. First we admitted we had a problem with anger. We admitted we had harmed others; we admitted we had harmed property; we admitted we had harmed ourselves. It was not easy. Most of us have felt the sting of guilt and shame, and often tried to escape those painful feelings by denying the harm we caused. We thought admitting our problem would only add to our feelings of low self-worth. But we took this crucial first step; otherwise, we could not have changed.

Principle Two: *We accept responsibility for our actions and will decide to stop our harmful behavior. We are willing to forgive those who harmed us, and to forgive ourselves for the harm we caused others.*

This, too, was a difficult principle. But we found we had to take this step. The guilt and shame we suffered because of our actions sometimes took us to the brink of suicide. We often blamed others for the results of our actions; that was our way of dealing with guilt and shame and of avoiding personal responsibility. Our avoidance behavior only resulted in another brick being placed in the wall of our denial.

Finally we faced reality. We accepted personal responsibility for our actions, and we accepted the negative consequences of our actions; then we were able to make a conscious decision to stop our harmful behavior.

To get the most from this principle, we had to add two more parts. Some of us had been severely hurt by others in the past. Some of us suffered from debilitating emotional effects of childhood trauma. But we could not move forward until we became willing to forgive those who harmed us. We found we also had to be willing to forgive ourselves. The act of forgiving ourselves was often much harder than forgiving others.

Principle Three: *We believe we are never justified in using violent words, threats, or actions to feel powerful over people, situations, or things.*

Finally we understood why we used anger, violence, and rage. Finally we understood why we repeated the same old pattern, even when we hated ourselves for our actions. Now we could move forward to a solution to the problem.

Finally we accepted the idea that verbal or physical violence was never justified. Having accepted that idea, we could move toward developing new ideas about the meaning of anger and to search and find non-violent ways to feel empowered.

Principle Four: *We are finding new ways to feel personal power that do not violate other people's right to feel safe.*

This Principle helped speed up our progress. We worked hard to learn new skills. What we learned led to feelings of personal power and influence that we could feel proud of instead of ashamed of. Some of us learned a more satisfying way to earn a living. Some of us went into business for ourselves. Some of us returned to school to learn a new trade or career. Some of us became professional counselors or therapists.

Principle Five: *We are committed to treating all people and their property with the dignity and respect that we, ourselves, deserve and expect.*

It was hard for some of us to put this Principle into practice. Some of us had been hurt badly. We often wished to retaliate; yet we decided we could no longer hold grudges. We knew we had to move forward, and we knew we had to let go of the pain of the past in order to do so.

Principle Six: *We are learning how negative beliefs fueled our anger. We are adopting new, empowering beliefs to take their place.*

We discovered that some of our beliefs kept us stuck; the ones that kept us stuck were negative beliefs. They limited us. We found we could discard those beliefs and could learn new beliefs—new beliefs that would help us change our angry behavior and keep it changed.

Principle Seven: *We believe we can change. And we believe we have a purpose beyond the gratification of our own personal desires.*

Many of us felt beyond help. We felt hopeless and helpless. We believed we could not change our violent behavior, and were doomed to continue hurting those we loved and to suffering further personal losses. We were greatly relieved when we found that we could change. The most empowering thing we learned was that we had a purpose. We learned that our mission could help us to grow in an astonishing way.

Principle Eight: *We are being transformed by working this program. Now we forgive those who harmed us and forgive ourselves; now we choose to continue our path of emotional, mental, and spiritual growth, and to help others find their pathway to peace.*

We practiced the Pathways to Peace principles. We went to Pathways to Peace meetings. We learned from each other. Then we discovered our lives are being transformed.

But we do not stop there. We continue to practice the Principles. We stay on the path. We keep growing and changing. We keep practicing forgiveness, perhaps the most difficult of all the things we are asked to do—and must do.

We are transformed. We feel obligated, even compelled, to help others who were driven by anger, rage, and violence.

The Eighth is the only one of the Pathways to Peace Principles that mentions the word "spirituality." We believe that a change of character must take place. Therefore we need to pay attention to the spiritual part of our whole self. We believe that all human beings need some form of spiritual connection. In that sense, Pathways to Peace is spiritual. However, we find it best to leave it up to each individual Pathways to Peace member to choose his or her own spiritual path. We want to be happily free of anger and rage; so we must follow a balanced path of change and growth at all vital levels of human functioning. Spirituality is one of the vital levels.

The Eighth Principle talks about *transformation*. Transformation means big change. When you transform, you change in a big way. You change your character. You change and grow at every part of your whole self. But transformation is a lifelong process, not a single event. Transformation requires life-long commitment and life-long growth in all eight parts of your whole self. Transformation is a journey.

The journey won't always be easy; things will get tough from time to time. Don't get discouraged, and never, never, never give up.

Pathways to Peace Rules

Here are the Pathways to Peace meeting rules. The rules assure the safety of the members:

1. Agree not to share information about group members outside the group.
2. Agree not to be violent at meetings.
3. Agree not to bring weapons to group.
4. Agree not to attend meetings under the influence of alcohol or other drugs.

The Pathways to Peace Mentor Program

Pathways to Peace has a mentor program. A mentor is a wise teacher, or trusted advisor. A mentor is sometimes called a "role model." A role model is someone who sets an example. A role model can set good examples or bad examples. A Pathways to Peace mentor (role model) is expected to set a good example.

The Pathways to Peace mentor program strengthens the power of the group. Pathways to Peace mentors help out new members. They are not counselors. They charge no fees.

The Pathways to Peace Principles—Short Version
To Be Read at Pathways to Peace Meetings

Principle One: We admit we have a problem with anger and have harmed people, property, and ourselves. Whenever possible, we will make amends or restitution.

Principle Two: We accept responsibility for our actions and will stop our harmful behavior. We are willing to forgive those who harmed us, and to forgive ourselves for the harm we caused others.

Principle Three: We believe we are never justified in using violent words, threats, or actions to feel powerful over people, situations, or things.

Principle Four: We are finding new ways to feel personal power that do not violate other people's right to feel safe.

Principle Five: We are committed to treating all people and their property with the dignity and respect that we, ourselves, deserve and expect.

Principle Six: We are learning how negative beliefs fuel our anger. We are adopting new, empowering beliefs to take their place.

Principle Seven: We believe we can change. And we believe we have a purpose beyond the gratification of our own personal desires.

Principle Eight: We are being transformed by working this program. Now we forgive those who harmed us and forgive ourselves; now we choose to continue our path of emotional, mental, and spiritual growth, and to help others find their pathway to peace.

Definition of Violence

Imagine a line stretching from wall to wall across a room. The left-hand wall represents verbal abuse: name calling, screaming and yelling, sarcasm, and verbal threats. Threatening postures and gestures belong somewhere near the center of the line. The right-hand wall represents physical violence which may result in injury or death.

It's all violence.

Copyright 2008
Pathways to Peace, Inc.

APPENDIX B

Starting a Pathways to Peace
Group in Your Area

Y ou have completed the *Managing Teen Anger and Violence* workbook. Now you will want to reinforce what you have learned, and share your knowledge with others. You will want to participate in a Pathways to Peace group in your area. If there are no groups in your area, you might want to start one. Setting up a group is not difficult. Here's how.

Find a Facilitator

First, find a responsible and knowledgeable adult to co-facilitate the group (perhaps someone from an adult PTP supervised group).

Find a Place to Meet

Then, you need a place to meet. Contact the places of worship in your area. Ask them if they could donate space. Human service agencies that do anger management counseling might help you find space.

Get the Word Out

Next, you will need to get the word out. Contact your local newspaper. Ask them to put an announcement in their calendar of events; there is usually no charge.

Shoppers' guides will usually place an announcement for you at no charge. In the announcement, simply say a Pathways to Peace group is forming. Mention that the group is free. Make sure to include the location and the day and time of the meeting. Give your phone number in the announcement and ask people to call for details.

Also, contact radio stations and cable TV stations. They often offer free public announcement services. Another good way to get the word out is to place flyers on supermarket bulletin boards. Get permission from the store manager to post some flyers. Twelve-Step groups (Alcoholics Anonymous or Narcotics Anonymous) would probably be willing to post some of your flyers at their meetings. You could even ask to start a Pathways to Peace group at the local jail. County probation offices are also good resources for spreading the word about your new group.

Refreshments

You may want to provide coffee or soft drinks at the meeting. If so, pass a basket for a small donation (one dollar or less) to help with costs. But be sure to get permission from the hosting facility to serve and/or prepare beverages.

Meeting Times

Evenings from 7:00 to 8:00 PM are usually the best meeting times for most people. It is difficult to get people to commit to a Pathways to Peace meeting on weekends or during daytime hours during the workweek.

It will take time and effort to get a Pathways to Peace group up and running in your area. It may cost a small amount of money. But the result will be more than worthwhile. You will have an opportunity to help yourself. You will have an opportunity to help other people—people like yourself; people who want to stop verbally or physically abusing family members; people who want to stop abusing friends, employers, pets, or even themselves; people who are stuck because they don't know where to turn. You can help. You have a new understanding of the nature of anger and rage. You have new skills. You can help provide a place for others to turn to for help.

Pathways to Peace Materials

In order to start a Pathways to Peace group, you will need a few materials. You will need at least one *Managing Teen Anger and Violence* workbook. You may order workbooks from Pathways to Peace, Inc. or from the publisher (see back of book).

However, you are asked not to copy any part of the workbook. The *Managing Teen Anger and Violence* workbook is copyrighted material. Each group member should purchase his or her own workbook. Sometimes when a member cannot afford to purchase a workbook, the group uses money from the basket containing donations to purchase a workbook for the member. Pathways to Peace groups may also purchase workbooks at the wholesale price, if a minimum of five workbooks are purchased at one time. Call Pathways to Peace for details (1-800-775-4212).

Pathways to Peace Group Structure Guidelines

Each Pathways to Peace group is composed of a volunteer primary facilitator, a volunteer assistant, participants, and at least one adult supervisor who attends all the meetings.

Primary Facilitator's Responsibilities

1. Locates meeting space.
2. Gets the word out (publicity).
3. Opens and closes meeting.
4. Sets up meeting, assisted by volunteers.
5. Keeps the physical space in proper order.
6. Passes the basket for donations at the end of meeting.
7. Communicates with Pathways to Peace main office.
8. Serves one to three months as facilitator.
9. Obtains and trains alternative facilitators.

Volunteer Assistant's Responsibilities

1. Helps facilitator set up meeting.
2. May make the coffee or prepare other beverages.
3. May act as facilitator when primary facilitator and sec./treas. are both absent.

Participant's Responsibilities

1. Be on time.
2. Comply with group rules.
3. Bring PTP workbook to meetings.

Pathways to Peace Meeting Facilitator's Guide

Introduction

The *Pathways to Peace Anger Management Workbook* is the official guidebook for adult Pathways to Peace programs. The *Managing Teen Anger and Violence* workbook should be used as the official guidebook for the teen groups. Pathways to

Peace group participants need to learn about the content of the workbook in order to help themselves and each other change their behavior and to grow.

At least some time should be spent reading from the workbook during each group session. Ideally, a group will read a part of each chapter during the hour the group meets. Ten to twenty minutes should be devoted to reading the workbook, during the first half-hour of the session. Groups should cycle through one reading of the entire workbook every six to eight months. Reading of the material should be voluntary. If a participant does not wish to read, he or she may simply say "Pass" or "I would rather not read today." No one should feel they are being forced to read.

After they read from the workbook during the first half hour of the group session, the second half hour should be opened up for comments from the participants. The facilitator should help the group focus their comments on the content of the workbook. Once the reading from the workbook has been completed, participants should also be encouraged to talk in a general way about personal issues that pertain to anger and rage. When discussion veers from the main purpose of the Pathways to Peace program and message, the facilitator should use the Pathways to Peace Eight Principles, Rules, and Definition of Violence to help the group refocus.

Using the workbook and the materials as the primary focus of the meetings will keep the group process from breaking down into "blame and complain" sessions.

Meeting Time: Approximately one hour.

1. Open meeting. Start by introducing yourself (first name only) to the group.

   "Hi everybody. My name is _____, and I have a problem with my anger." Then, starting on your right or left, go around the group and have everyone else introduce themselves by their first name and tell why they are at the meeting.

2. Guide members through a brief relaxation exercise to help them reduce their stress level. Take about 30 seconds. Speak slowly, using a soft tone.

   "Take a deep breath in, then a deep breath out and relax your posture. Continuing to breathe in a relaxed way, slowly and deeply, reflect on how important it is to learn how to relax in this way. Practice this skill several times a day, until it becomes a part of you. Use this technique whenever you feel stressed or whenever you feel an anger trigger of any kind."

3. Ask a member to read the Pathways to Peace Principles (turn to pages 230 and 231).

4. Ask a member to read the Rules on page 230.

5. Ask a member to read the Definition of Violence on page 232.

6. Make any announcements that would be of interest to the group.

7. Go directly to whatever workbook chapter the group is studying. Go around the room, starting on your left or right, and ask for volunteers to read a page or two from the chapter. Do not stop to do the exercises in the group, unless the group has decided to do so. Ask the participants to complete the written work on their own time, before the group meets again. Ask members if they have any questions about the materials just read. If so, encourage members to help each other find the appropriate answers. Refer to the workbook, or to the Principles, Rules, or Definition of Violence, when confusion occurs.

8. Ask members if they have any problems or issues having to do with anger, that have come up over the past week and that they would like some feedback about from the group. Start on your right or left, and give each person a chance to comment. Participants who do not wish to comment may simply say "I pass" or "I don't want to comment tonight." Those who wish to comment should be allowed 2-5 minutes to speak. Then go to the next person. Do not allow a few individuals to take up most of the time. Participants may comment more than once if everyone else has been given an opportunity to comment.

9. Approximately two minutes before ending the meeting, pass the basket for donations. (This is voluntary. No one should be made to feel they have to donate, and no one should put more than a dollar in the basket.)

10. Close the meeting with the following meditation:

"Everyone sit back and get into a more relaxed posture again. Take a slow, deep breath. Maintaining that more relaxed posture, continue to breathe slowly and deeply. Be aware for a moment or two of all the angry people all over the world, and of what they have lost because of their anger and rage. Some of them have lost their families; some have lost their jobs; some have lost their freedom, or their self-respect. Some have even lost their lives.

"Be aware also of all of the victims of other people's anger and rage, and recognize they don't deserve the pain they are going through.

"Be aware that it doesn't have to be that way for us anymore. We can meet together as we have today, and help each other find new ways to deal with our triggers—new ways that do not violate other people's right to feel safe.

"Above all, recognize that everybody in this room deserves to be happy, as long as it is not at someone else's expense. Have a good week, everybody. See you next week."

11. Before leaving the meeting site, make sure everything is in order (lights off, water taps off, room back in order, trash cleaned up, etc.).

If You Need Assistance

If you need help starting or facilitating a group, or if you wish to order additional Pathways to Peace workbooks, call Pathways to Peace (1-800-775-4212). We will be glad to do what we can to assist you.

Pathways to Peace

PO Box 259, Cassadaga, NY 14718

1-800-775-4212

Email: transfrm@netsync.net

www.pathwaystopeaceinc.com

INDEX

THE AUTHOR

William Fleeman is the author of three books: *The Pathways to Peace Anger Management Workbook* (Hunter House, 2003), *The Pathways to Sobriety Workbook* (Hunter House, 2004), and *Managing Teen Anger and Violence* (Impact Publications, 2008).

Bill is the founder of Pathways to Peace, Inc., a nonprofit self-help program for anger management and violence prevention. This growing organization has groups in the United States and Canada. Pathways to Peace in-house groups also are in prisons, chemical dependency agencies, and probation departments.

Two of Bill's books, *The Pathways to Peace Anger Management Workbook* and *Managing Teen Anger and Violence*, are the official guidebooks for the Pathways to Peace program.

Bill also writes and markets alcoholism and substance abuse distance learning courses for chemical dependency counselors, which have been approved throughout the United States.

His video, *The Niagara Falls Metaphor*, is used by institutions and agencies throughout the U.S. and Canada. The video compares anger and rage to a trip down the Niagara River and over the Falls.

Bill lives peacefully in New York with his wife Janet and their cat, Shadow.

By William Fleeman
Resources for Pathways to Peace Programs

Managing Teen Anger and Violence:
A Pathways to Peace Program
2008 | ISBN 1-57023-276-8 | $19.95

Pathways to Sobriety Workbook
2004 | ISBN 0-89793-417-2 | $24.95

The Pathways to Peace Anger Management Workbook
2003 | ISBN 0-89793-427-X | $24.95

The Niagara Falls Metaphor Program
2002 | DVD or VHS formats | $69.95

Also From Impact Publications

Angry Men:
Managing Anger in an Unforgiving World
2004 | ISBN 1-57023-205-9 | $14.95

Angry Women: Stop Letting
Anger Control Your Life!
2004 | ISBN 1-57023-206-7 | $14.95

Anger and Conflict in the Workplace:
Spot the Signs, Avoid the Trauma
2003 | ISBN 1-57023-138-9 | $15.95

ORDER THROUGH:

IMPACT PUBLICATIONS
9104-N Manassas Drive, Manassas Park, VA 20111
Tel: 800-361-1055; Fax: 703-335-9486; online: www.impactpublications.com

The **Ultimate** *Re-Entry Success Guides for*
Ex-Offenders!

Ex-Offender's Job Hunting Guide

Ron and Caryl Krannich, Ph.Ds

Ex-offenders face special challenges when looking for employment, from identifying ex-offender-friendly employers to handling difficult interview questions about their backgrounds, goals, and accomplishments. Like a trusted friend or counselor, this comprehensive book helps ex-offenders develop the proper attitudes and strategies for landing jobs that can lead to rewarding long-term careers. Individual chapters address such important issues as attitudes, motivations, goals, research, networking, applications, resumes, cover letters, interviews, and starting a new job. Covers the psychological adjustments of ex-offenders as well as includes a special section on community-based organizations and services designed to assist ex-offenders in transition. Rich with examples, tests, and exercises to help ex-offenders develop a plan of action for ensuring success in today's job market. 2005. 7 x 10. 224 pages. ISBN 1-57023-236-9. $17.95

Ex-Offender's Quick Job Hunting Guide

Ron and Caryl Krannich, Ph.Ds

This companion workbook for The Ex-Offender's Job Hunting Guide is filled with practical tests and exercises for organizing and implementing 10 steps for re-entering the work world. Includes special sections on improving the quality of questions and changing attitudes and behaviors. 2006. 128 pages. 7 x 10. ISBN 1-57023-250-4. $9.95.

Best Resumes and Letters for Ex-Offenders

Wendy S. Enelow and Ronald L. Krannich, Ph.D.

Finally, a resume guide that addresses special employment issues facing ex-offenders. Written by two of America's leading career experts, this book includes sound advice on how to write, produce, distribute, and follow up resumes and letters. Includes 85 examples of outstanding resumes and letters written for ex-offenders. Includes a special chapter on questions frequently asked by ex-offenders about finding a job. 2006. 212 pages. 7 x 10. ISBN 1-57023-251-2. $19.95.

Stay Out for Good!
Job Finding Kit

Here's the ultimate collection of books designed to assist ex-offenders in finding jobs and staying out for good. Can purchase separately.

SPECIAL: $199.95 for complete set of 18 books (plus shipping).

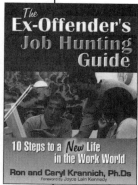

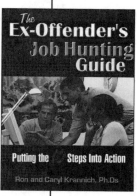

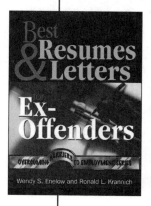

- *9 to 5 Beats Ten to Life* ($15.00)
- *99 Days and a Get Up* ($9.95)
- *America's Top 100 Jobs for People Without a Four-Year Degree* ($19.95)
- *America's Top Jobs for People Re-Entering the Workforce* ($19.95)
- *Best Resumes and Letters for Ex-Offenders* ($19.95)
- *The Ex-Offender's Job Hunting Guide* ($17.95)
- *Ex-Offender's Job Search Companion* ($11.95)
- *The Ex-Offender's Quick Job Hunting Guide* ($9.95)
- *Job Hunting Tips for People With Hot and Not-So-Hot Backgrounds* ($17.95)
- *Job Interview Tips for People With Not-So-Hot Backgrounds* ($14.95)
- *Man, I Need a Job* ($7.95)
- *No One Will Hire Me!* ($15.95)
- *Putting the Bars Behind You* (6 books, $57.95)

For information on these and other resources (videos, DVDs, software, posters, games, assessment instruments, special value kits, downloadable catalogs and flyers) relevant to ex-offenders and re-entry success, visit ***www.impactpublications.com***.

How to Order: Impact Publications, 9104-N Manasssas Drive, VA 20111, Tel. 1-800-361-1055, Fax 703-335-9486, or email: query@impactpublications.com

Your One-Stop Career, Life Skills, and Travel Centers

Books, DVDs, posters, games, pamphlets, and articles on anger management, addiction, recovery, mental health, jobs, careers, education, travel, military, ex-offenders, and much more!

www.impactpublications.com

www.exoffenderreentry.com

www.veteransworld.com

www.ishoparoundtheworld.com